New County Series

£ 2-00

RAN

Gwynedd

/34

A Guide to North-west Wales

ROBIN CLARK

First published in Great Britain 1978
by Robin Clark Ltd., 15 Leyden Road,
Stevenage, Herts, SG1 2BW

Made and printed in Great Britain by
M C Print Co. Ltd., Stevenage, Herts.

ISBN 0 86072 013 6

CONTENTS

ILLUSTRATIONS

ACKNOWLEDGEMENTS

So many people have contributed to my knowledge of the legends, history and literature of Gwynedd during the many years I have wandered there that it is impossible to acknowledge them all individually. Most of them have been mentioned in my previous books on Wales, and all too many have since died, including my husband, Edgar Phillips (Trefîn), and Sir Cynan Jones (Cynan), but I must mention especially Mr. and Mrs. Grove-White of Brynddu, Llanfechell, who last year kindly showed me over the house and garden associated with William Bulkeley, which is not normally open to the public. I am also indebted to Miss Mary Pearce for reading the proofs, and the Wales Tourist Board and the British Tourist Authority for some of the photographs. The others are from my own collection.

Maxwell Fraser

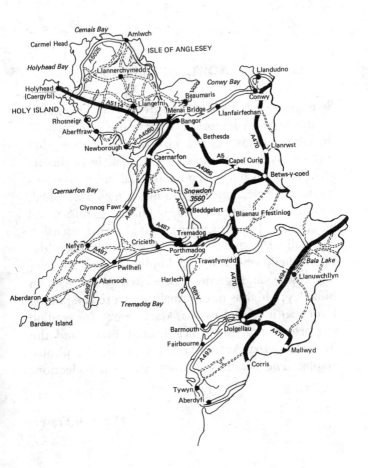

INTRODUCTION

The administrative area of Gwynedd, which came into being in 1974, is made up of the counties of Môn (Anglesey) and Caernarfonshire, the greater part of Meirionydd, and a small area of Denbighshire on the east bank of Afon Conwy. The name is that of the old Welsh kingdom of Gwynedd.

Two-thirds of the population of Gwynedd is Welsh-speaking - a higher proportion than in any other part of Wales. The Gwynedd County Council, alone among local authorities of Great Britain, holds bi-lingual meetings, with instant translations for the benefit of those councillors and rate-payers who cannot speak Welsh. All documents are issued in both Welsh and English.

Gwynedd has been a haunt of holiday-makers, tourists and sportsmen ever since the Lake Poets discovered the attraction of mountains. Now the roads of the old Welsh cattle-drovers, who flourished from the 15th century until the coming of the railways, are ideal for pony trekking; the once flourishing slate quarries are a tourist attraction, and the narrow-gauge railways have been revived by enthusiastic amateurs. Numerous Welsh woollen mills now open their doors to visitors, and handcrafts are thriving in many towns and villages.

The larger resorts have their indoor and outdoor entertainments, but Gwynedd is, above all, a county for those who love beautiful scenery and open air activities, with no large industries to pollute the atmosphere, a background of legend and history, and the heart-warming hospitality of the Welsh people.

Although the mountains of Caernarfonshire and

Meirionydd cannot compare in height with the Himalayas and other great ranges of the world, they rise so sheerly from sea level that they are far more impressive than their measurements suggest, and they have been the subject of many famous paintings and poems.

Snowdonia, which was the stronghold and refuge of the Welsh princes of Gwynedd until their final overthrow by Edward I, is now a part of the Snowdonia National Park which covers almost the whole of Caernarfonshire and Meirionydd, as far south as the Dyfi estuary, which marks the boundary between North and South Wales. Meirionydd's mountains have a character quite distinct from those of Caernarfonshire, and the Cadair Idris range is second only to the Snowdon group in popularity.

Cardigan Bay, the remote peninsula of Lleyn, and the estuaries of the Dyfi, Mawddach and Glaslyn give diversity to mainland Gwynedd. The Isle of Anglesey, although less obviously beautiful, has a fascination which escapes travellers who hurry across the island by road or rail, for it must be sought in a more leisurely fashion. The coastline on the east and north is magnificent and there are many small woodlands surviving from the days when Anglesey was so thickly wooded that the bards described it as 'the shady isle'. Holyhead Mountain (Mynydd Twr), the highest mountain, is only just over 700 ft., but there are many unexpected little hills and valleys, and the peaks of Snowdonia are seldom out of sight.

Gerald de Barri (Giraldus Cambrensis, or Gerald the Welshman) wrote in his *Itinerary Through Wales* in the 12th century: '. . . this island is incomparably more fertile in corn than any other part of Wales, from whence arose the British proverb " 'Môn, mam Cymry', Mona mother of Wales"; and when the crops have been defective in all other parts of the country, this island, from the richness of its soil and abundant produce, has been able to supply all Wales'. Anglesey is still the most fertile area of Gwynedd.

Some of the finest and largest castles in Great Britain

are to be found in Gwynedd. Most are under the care of the Department of the Environment and open to the public. The Department also preserves the remains of Cymer Abbey, Gwydir Uchaf Chapel, Penarth Fawr medieval hall and a large number of the many prehistoric monuments.

The opening hours of the buildings and gardens owned by the National Trust are advertised in the list issued annually by the Trust, and also locally. A very few of the Tudor, Georgian and 19th century houses in private ownership can be viewed if written permission is obtained beforehand, but the majority are closed to the public.

The churches of Gwynedd are mostly of very early foundation, and of great simplicity externally. Even when they have been enlarged and restored, the exterior remains plain. There are few towers, and even fewer spires, and often only a single bell-cot distinguishes a church from a barn, giving little hint of the wealth of woodwork, stone carving, effigies and memorials frequently to be found within. Unfortunately, increasing vandalism has necessitated locking many churches when no service is being held, and in the case of some of the most ancient and interesting churches in remote districts services are held only once a year and enquiries should be made before a visit regarding the whereabouts of keys.

The indigenous architecture of farms, cottages and villages has the rugged strength of walls of huge, rough-hewn stones and slate roofs which blend with the mountain setting, but Gwynedd does not dwell solely in the past. Among modern developments are hydro-electric plants, nuclear power stations, a marine oil terminal, and a multipurpose British Rail Ferry service opened in 1977.

The geology of Gwynedd is of exceptional interest. There are pre-Cambrian rocks in Anglesey, and to a lesser degree in outcrops in Caernarfonshire, which represent the ancient high land worn down until the old ribs scarcely protrude above the general level, affording the greatest proportion of arable land. The Cambrian system on the mainland includes the huge beds of slate which made the fortunes of quarry-owners in the 18th and 19th centuries, and Ordovician igneous rocks form the most imposing mountain groups of Wales. Minor elements of the scenery were modified in the Glacial Period which left spectacular evidence of the overwhelming power of the ice. Finally, the raising of the sea-level along the Welsh coast when the ice melted is reflected in the many legends of lost cities in Cardigan Bay and the Lavan Sands.

The prehistory and archaeology of Wales is similar to that of the whole of England, for the Welsh are the descendants of the 'Ancient Britons' of Caesar's day. They were driven into the area now known as Wales by the invading Saxons, who called them 'Wealhas' or foreigners. It was during this period that the Welsh began calling themselves Cymry (fellow countrymen) and that the legends of Arthur grew up.

At the time of the Roman invasion Anglesey and the north-west of Wales were inhabited by the Venedotae, who are believed to have spoken an Irish dialect and to have had little in common with the Ordovices in the south of Gwynedd. After the Romans left Britain - possibly at the beginning of the 5th century - Cunedda, a Romano-British chieftain, came down from Manaw Gododdin (Strathclyde) with his sons and warriors, and began driving the Venedotae back to Ireland. He founded the dynasty of Gwynedd which was destined to play a prominent part in Welsh history.

Gwynedd was one of the four great kingdoms of Wales, the others being Powys in the north-east, Deheubarth in the south-west and Morgannwg in the south-east. Although their boundaries fluctuated with the fortunes of war, growing larger under a powerful ruler and contracting under a weak one, and sometimes breaking up into a number of smaller kingdoms, these four persisted until the Edwardian conquest in the 13th century.

Each of the kingdoms was divided into regions called cantrefs (Hundreds) and each cantref was subdivided into two, three or more commotes, the leading feature of which was its court, for the trial of disputes between free tribesmen.

Outstanding among direct descendants of Cunedda was his great grandson, Maelgwn Gwynedd, a strong and able ruler. He was in conflict from time to time with contemporary saints, including St. Cybi of Holyhead, but invariably ended by giving them lands and concessions. Under the name of Maglocunus he was among the Welsh princes attacked by Gildas, who appears to have thought Maelgwn received his deserts for abandoning his monastic vows when he died of the plague about 547.

Nothing is known of Cadfan, whose tombstone has survived at Llangadwaladr, but his son and successor, Cadwallon, who defeated Edwin of Northumbria in 633, and died in the same year, became the hero of many legends. He was succeeded by his son, Cadwaladr. Nothing is known of his deeds, but he must have been a notable figure in his day for it was prophesied of him, as of King Arthur, that he would return in the hour of need to lead his people to victory.

Henry VII claimed descent from Cadwaladr, and the red dragon of Cadwaladr was one of the three standards he offered up in St. Paul's in 1485. Cadwaladr died in the great plague of 664. It seems probable that at the close of his life he became a monk. The church of Llangadwaladr claims him as its patron saint and founder, and churches are dedicated to him in other parts of Wales.

Cadwaladr's successors were undistinguished, and the last of the direct line, Hywel ap Rhodri Molwynog, died in 825. Merfyn Frych (the Freckled), who inherited through the female line, was the son of Gwriad (believed to have been a Manx chieftain), and maintained his position for 19 years through sheer force of character.

When he died in 844 he was able to hand over to his son Rhodri the whole of his territories unimpaired.

Rhodri Mawr (the Great) afterwards inherited two other Welsh kingdoms, and by the time of his death in 877 he ruled nearly all Wales. Unfortunately, this unity subsequently disintegrated, but Rhodri's achievements gave the Welsh people their first vision of national unity. He imbued them with such veneration for his name that every later prince who aspired to national leadership found his best claim to the love and loyalty of the Welsh was based on descent from Rhodri. He was a contemporary of Alfred of England and both deserve the title of Great. They alone organized the forces of their respective countries against the hordes of Danish invaders and were successful in bringing a period of peace to their war ravaged lands.

One of the most memorable of Rhodri's successors was Gruffydd ap Cynan, the only one of the earlier Welsh princes about whom a biography was written. Although the earliest known copy dates from 150 years after his death, there is reason to believe it was originally written during the reign of his son, Owain Gwynedd. Gruffydd had many difficulties to contend with in his early career, but when he died peacefully in 1137 at the age of 82, he was undisputed ruler of a kingdom stretching eastward to the Clwyd, and on the south to the borders of Deheubarth. He is buried in Bangor cathedral.

Gruffydd's lifetime coincided with the fiercest Norman attacks on Wales, but he gave his country many years of peace, and an old chronicler says that his kingdom 'shone with lime-washed churches like the firmament with the stars'. These churches and his principal royal residences have been rebuilt or have fallen into ruin, but a doorway of Aberffraw church is believed to be a relic of his work. He also introduced new musical methods, and encouraged a great revival of Welsh literature.

Owain, eldest son of Gruffydd ap Cynan, succeeded to the throne of Gwynedd on his father's death and, in order to distinguish him from Owain ap Gruffydd of the royal line of Powys, the unusual device of a territorial designation was adopted for both, the former becoming known as Owain Gwynedd, and the latter as Owain Cyfeiliog.

Owain Gwynedd had that rare combination of great courage, energy, wisdom, prudence and good luck which makes a successful leader. Although Henry II led an expedition against him, it was such a fiasco that no further attempt was made to subjugate Wales until after Owain's death in 1170. He, too, was buried in Bangor cathedral.

It was during Owain Gwynedd's reign, about 1154, that the titles of king and prince were dropped by other Welsh rulers for the less provocative title of lord, and only the rulers of Gwynedd retained the title of prince, by an apparently general agreement.

One of the greatest Welsh poems of the 12th century was composed by Gwalchmai, chief bard of Gwynedd, in honour of Owain Gwynedd. It was translated into English by Thomas Gray, under the name of *The Triumphs of Owen.*

The national revival continued to flower into a rich and varied literature and there was a rapid spread of monasticism with the princes founding and endowing monasteries and encouraging the religious fervour of their people.

The two Llywelyns between them span almost the whole of the 13th century. The first 40 years saw the rise of Llywelyn ab Iorweth (Llywelyn Fawr: the Great), grandson of Owain Gwynedd, to supreme power, and the close of the century saw the death of Llywelyn ap Gruffydd (Y Llyw Olaf: Llywelyn the Last) and the extinguishing of Welsh independence by Edward I.

Llywelyn Fawr wielded greater power in Wales than any other prince had done since the Norman Conquest of England, but he never claimed the title of Prince of Wales. It was his pride to be recognized as Prince of

Aberffraw and Lord of Snowdon. He spent his last years building up the prosperity of his country, and was an enlightened friend of the movement for religious reform. Hot tempered, but never bigoted or hidebound, he was always ready to consider and, if necessary, adopt new ideas.

Literature flourished in a new springtime of glorious poetry and prose. It was during his lifetime that the earliest known text of the Four Branches of *The Mabinogion* - that storehouse of Welsh legends - was written down. He died in the abbey of Aberconwy in 1290, and was buried there.

Llywelyn Fawr was succeeded by his son Dafydd, who proved unable to consolidate the work of his father, but after his death in 1248 Llywelyn ap Gruffydd, the most able of the grandsons of Llywelyn Fawr, set himself to achieve supreme power in Wales. By 1267 he had reached a height of authority and influence greater than that of any previous ruler, and assumed the title of Prince of Wales.

There was peace in the land for a while but he was not so wise and tactful as his grandfather and in the nature of things the peace could not last. The struggle with England was intensified on the accession of Edward I in 1272 and finally Llywelyn was starved out of even the last traditional refuge of the Welsh in Snowdonia. He was hunted down and killed near Builth Wells in 1282 and his head was sent to London, to be fixed on a pole at the Tower with a crown of ivy on it in mockery. His princely coronet was offered up at the shrine of Edward the Confessor in Westminster Abbey, and the famous Croes Naid, or Croes Neyt, believed to be a piece of the True Cross, and one of the most cherished possessions of Llywelyn and his ancestors, was also brought to London in much the same spirit as the Stone of Scone was later brought from Scotland. The Croes Naid disappeared during the Civil War but a representation of it can be seen on a boss in St. George's Chapel, Windsor Castle.

Edward I passed the Statute of Rhuddlan in 1284 which carved the kingdom of Gwynedd into the counties of Anglesey, Caernarfonshire and Meirionydd and established new laws restricting Welsh freedom.

The greatest and most far-reaching of the disturbances in Wales after the death of Llywelyn the Last was the revolt of Owain Glyndŵr, at the beginning of the 15th century. The immediate cause was a personal feud between Owain Glyndŵr and the English baron, Lord Grey of Ruthin, but it gained support through the ever-increasing resentment of the Welsh against the oppression and extortion practised unceasingly and unsparingly by the tax gatherers of the English Crown.

Even greater repression and poverty for the Welsh followed the defeat of Glyndŵr, and it was not until Henry Tudor ascended the English throne as Henry VII that laws against the Welsh were relaxed.

There are varying opinions of the date when Christianity was introduced into Britain but it is on record that three British bishops were present at the Synod of Arles in 314 and at the Council of Ariminus in 359 and at other Councils in the 5th and 6th centuries until the Saxon invaders cut off direct communication between the Celtic Church and the Church of Rome.

Monasticism was introduced about 420 A.D. and the 'Age of Saints' followed. Many legends gathered around the memory of the saints but very few facts are known beyond the sites of the churches they founded, or which were dedicated in their honour. It is clear, however, that the early church in Britain was extremely well organized and flourishing and held in repute far beyond these shores when the Saxon invasion began in 449, and it remained a strong influence in Wales throughout the troubled times which followed. When Augustine landed in England in 597 on his mission to the pagan Saxons, the Welsh saints were venerated, monasteries and churches were flourishing all over Wales and Welsh missionaries had done lasting work in Cornwall, Brittany and Ireland, although they do not seem to have attempted to convert the hated Saxons.

The Celtic Church remained completely orthodox on the vital matter of doctrine but divergent practices had grown up during the separation from Rome. The Celtic Church observed Easter according to the system adopted by the Council of Arles in 314, while Rome had adopted the Table of Dionysius. There was another difference of opinion over the form of tonsure. The Roman Catholic monks shaved the top of the head; the Celtic monks had adopted a frontal tonsure. Sir John Rhys thought it was 'probably a druidic tonsure continued', the druidical tonsure being effected by shaving all the hair in front of a line drawn over the crown of the head from ear to ear.

Among other and more serious differences the Celtic Church permitted clergy, including bishops, abbots and saints, to marry and allowed hereditary succession to abbacies. The Roman Catholic church permitted neither. Also, there were no Archbishops, and the Celtic bishops, unlike those of Rome, exercised their influence solely through their own reputation for holiness and had no territorial powers.

It was not until 768 that Easter observances were altered in Wales. The last Celtic usage, that of married clergy, did not disappear until 1138. The Welsh Church, in spite of constant pressure, was not brought into complete submission to Canterbury until after the magnificent fight by Giraldus Cambrensis on behalf of its complete freedom finally ended in failure in 1203. The Welsh Church then lost its independence, and did not regain it for over 700 years.

GLOSSARY OF SOME OF THE WORDS OCCURRING IN WELSH PLACE-NAMES

Note: Some initial consonants (b, c, d, g, ll, m, p, rh, t) are mutated under certain conditions

ABER, the confluence of a tributary river with the main stream, or a place where a river flows into the sea.

ADWY, gap or pass

AFON, river

ALLT, wooded hill or cliff

ARAN, high place

BACH, little

BAN, (pl. bannau), peak or highland

BANC, platform, tableland

BEDD, a grave

BEDW, birch, BEDWAS, place of birches

BETWS, bede-house

BLAEN, end, point or head of vale or river

BOD, abode or dwelling

BRON, the slope of a hill

BRYN, mound or hill

BWLCH, pass or gap

BYCHAN, small, lesser

CAD, host, battle

CADAIR, chair, stronghold or seat

CAER, camp or fortress

CANOL, the middle

CANTREF, division of land, a hundred

CAPEL, chapel

CARN, a prominence

CARREG, a stone or rock

CASTELL, castle or fortress

CEFN, ridge

CELLI, grove or copse

CIL, recess or retreat

CLOGWEN, precipice, crag

COCH, red

COED, wood

CORS, bog or marshy place

CRAIG, or GRAIG, crag or rock

CROES, cross

CRUG, heap or mound

CWM, valley

CYMER, junction or confluence

DERWEN (pl. DERW) oak(s)

DIN or DINAS, town or hill fort

DÔL, meadow

DRWS, door

DU, black

DWFR or DŴR, water

17

DYFFRYN, vale or valley
EGLWYS, church
EPYNT, horse-track
ERCH, pale colour, terrible
ERW, acre
ERYRI, high mountain land
ESGAIR, long ridge
FFYNNON, well or spring
GARTH, hill or headland
GLAN, bank or shore
GLAS, blue if water, green if fields
GLYN, glen
GWAUN, moor or common
GWERN, swamp or bog
GWYN, GWEN, white
HAFOD, summer dwelling
HEN, old
HENDRE, main or winter residence
HIR, long
IS, lower
ISAF, lowest
ISEL, low
LLAM, leap
LLAN, enclosed place, or church, or village near a church
LLECH, flat stone
LLECHWEDD, hillside
LLETHR, slope
LLWYD, grey or venerable
LLWYN, grove
LLYN, lake

LLYS, court, hall, or palace
MAEN, stone
MAES, field
MAN, place
MAWR, great, large
MELIN, mill
MELYN, yellow
MERTHYR, martyr
MOEL, bare hill
MÔR, sea
MORFA, sea-marsh
MUR, wall
MWYN, mine, ore
MYNACH, monk
MYNYDD, mountain
NANT, brook
NEUADD, hall
NOS, night
OGOF, cave
ONN (pl. Ynn) ash tree
PANDY, (pl. pandau) fulling mill
PANT, hollow place or valley
PEN, head or top
PENMAEN, rocky place or headland
PENNANT, upper reaches of a glen
PISTYLL, cataract
PLAS, hall, place
PONT, bridge
PORTH, port or gate
PRIDD, soil
PWLL, pool, pit or hollow
RHAEADR, waterfall
RHIW, slope or ascent

18

RHOS, open moor
RHYD, ford
SAETH, arrow
SARN, causeway or pavement
SYCH, dry
TAL, tall, high
TAN, under, beneath
TIR, land, soil
TOMEN, heap, mound
TRAETH, shore, beach
TRAWS, cross
TRE or TREF, dwelling-place or village
TYDDYN, farmstead
TŶ (pl. TAI) house
UCHAF, highest, uppermost
UWCH, above, higher
Y, YR, the, of the
YN, YM, in
YNYS, island
YSBYTY, or YSPYTTY, hospital, or place or refreshment
YSGOL, school, or ladder
YSGOR, rampart or defence
YSTRAD, low, flat plain by a river
YSTUM, shape, form or curve
YSTWYTH, winding, or flexible

SIR FÔN (ANGLESEY)

ABERFFRAW is a remote village of south-west Anglesey, at the head of the narrow estuary of the Afon Ffraw. An 18th century hump-backed packhorse bridge spans the river, and sturdy stone houses are set well back from the banks where geese wander freely and crop the grass to a smooth expanse of green. Even the small Council estate has been planned with great care to blend with the older cottages of this attractive place.

The huge area of dunes which has surrounded Aberffraw for centuries is being planted with conifers by the Forestry Commission, and the whole character of the landscape is being transformed. A mile away the estuary broadens into Aberffraw Bay where pale, silvery sands edge the rock-bound coast. South-east is the vast expanse of the Malltraeth estuary and northward, past the primitive mother church of Llangwyfan, are prehistoric burial chambers to hint at the long ages during which this area has been populated.

St. Cwyfan was a follower of the Powysian St. Beuno, whose cult was strong in Gwynedd. Pilgrimages were made to Llangwyfan in earlier times but now services are held there only once a year in June, when the sun streams through the windows to light the simple 12th century church built on the 7th century foundations of the oratory. St. Cwyfan's was carefully restored in 1893. The islet can be reached by a causeway at low tide but is cut off at high spring tides. It is strewn with cowrie shells and pervaded by the mournful cry of curlews, and there is a sense of timelessness and solitude which not even the

Ministry of Defence establishment on a neighbouring headland has been able to destroy.

Directly north is Cable Bay (Porth Trecastell) which derives its English name from the Atlantic cable which ends there, and its Welsh name from a prehistoric fort on the cliffs. Here, too, is the Barcloddiad y Gawres, on a lonely site above the seashore. It is of special interest for the ornamentation on five of its stones. Bryn-celli-ddu, 10 miles away, is the only other known burial chamber in the United Kingdom in which megalithic mural art is preserved, but the Barcloddiad incised ornamentation has closer affinities with those found on the banks of the Boyne in Ireland. It has a passage 20 feet in length leading into a central burial chamber, with side chambers on the south and west, and was originally roofed and enclosed in a mound about 90 feet in diameter, of which the remains can be seen. Din Dryfol, a mile and a half north-east of Aberffraw, is on the right bank of the Afon Gwna. The chamber has been wrecked and only a few stones remain.

To English visitors Aberffraw is a typical Anglesey village which they may possibly associate with the Welsh shortbreads known as Aberffraw cakes, which are - or should be - baked in scallop shells; but to Welsh visitors Aberffraw is a place of glorious memories.

Here Branwen, daughter of King Lear (Llŷr) the mythical founder of London, who married Matholwch, King of Ireland, was acclaimed as the 'fairest maiden in the world', and here Cadfan was acknowledged King. Ten of his successors reigned at Aberffraw, ending with the death of the last Llywelyn, in 1282.

Life at Aberffraw in the days of the Princes, and their lavish hospitality, is described in *Llys Aberffraw* by my late husband Trefin (Archdruid of Wales), which is included in the *Oxford Book of Welsh Verse*. Unfortunately it is impossible to translate it adequately, as an English version of Welsh alliterative poetry cannot reproduce the brilliance of the internal consonantal rhyming which is a special feature of cywyddau (Welsh lyric poems).

The llys (court, or palace) was raided time and again, and was as frequently rebuilt, but nothing now remains - not even the site is known. St. Beuno's church in the village, with a fine 12th century blocked doorway, a 14th century font and an arcade, was much restored in the Victorian era. The wayside chapel of St. Mary's, Tal-y-llyn, three miles north, near Llyn Padrig, is more satisfying in the sturdy simplicity of its nave, dating from the 12th century, with 14th century additions, a late 16th century chancel and a 17th century south chapel. The pews are of planks halved over the wall footings and one of them is dated 1786. The communion rails date from the 18th century. St. Mary's is now disused but has been sympathetically restored by the Friends of Friendless Churches, and the Anglesey County Council.

AMLWCH. Although Amlwch has little history, and its only notable building provokes controversy rather than admiration, it has a superb situation on the rugged, unspoiled coastline of north-east Anglesey. There were only six houses there in 1766, but by 1801, Amlwch had over a thousand and a population of some 6,000, due to the development of the copper mines of Parys Mountain, a high tableland sheltering Amlwch on the landward side.

The mines were worked by the indefatigable Romans and possibly by earlier Bronze Age settlers. They were revived during the Tudor period for a while but had their greatest productivity in the late 18th century when they were developed jointly by the Parys Mine Company and the Mona Mine Company, under the active direction of Thomas Williams, an attorney born at Cefn Coch, in the parish of Llansadwrn, who was a partner in both companies. His success was phenomenal. Not only were immense quantities of copper exported, but numerous subsidiary concerns were set up, using such by-products as ochre, sulphur, alkali and alum. Clog-making and tobacco-processing also flourished. Smelting furnaces were developed at Amlwch, Holywell in Flintshire and at Swansea in South Wales, and by 1800 half the copper industry of the United Kingdom was in his hands.

During the peak period of the mine 1,500 men, women and children excavated 80,000 tons of good ore each year, and nearly nine million Amlwch penny tokens were issued. Parys Mountain became an outstanding attraction for every North Wales tourist, and such artists as Sandby and Ibbetson drew pictures of the miners at work.

Williams bought the mansion of Plas Llanidan and became the virtual director of the world's copper industry. He is still remembered as 'The Copper King', but it is less well known that he also did much to promote and improve turnip culture, which had been introduced into Anglesey in 1714, and that his nick-name in the Island to the end of his life was 'Twm Chware Teg' (Tom Fair Play). His descendants, several of whom married into the peerage, did not share his interest in the mines and are better remembered as the founders of banks.

The mines declined in the second half of the 19th century, although yellow ochre was still produced from the copper deposits. Some prospecting has been carried out from time to time but Parys Mountain to-day remains a strange, deserted area of dangerous shafts and bleak stretches of abandoned open-cast mining, strangely like a lunar landscape, even in bright sunshine.

The parish church, dedicated to the 6th century St. Elaeth, was built by the Mining Company in 1800 to replace an earlier church. Gravestones in the churchyard reflect the range of employment arising from the prosperity of the mines - smelters, coal merchants, surgeons, ships' captains, an Assay Master and a bookbinder, among others. Ffynnon Elaeth is in Amlwch Port, which is now joined up with Amlwch.

The Mining Company blasted the long narrow harbour of Amlwch Port out of solid rock for the export of their copper, and a ship-building yard was also set up.

Menai Suspension Bridge, the Isle of Anglesey's link with the mainland, was built by Thomas Telford and opened on 30th January 1826.

Photo: Wales Tourist Board

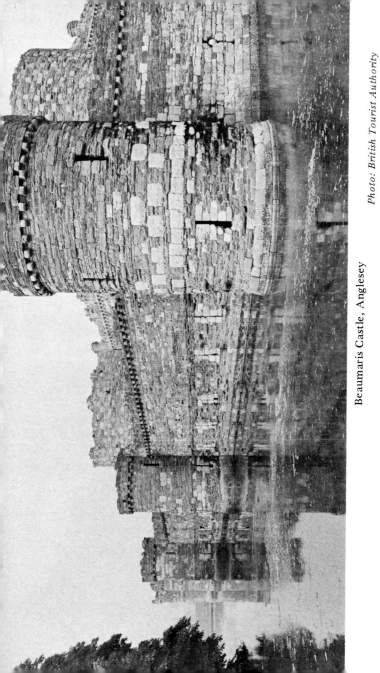

Beaumaris Castle, Anglesey

The last ship built there was launched in 1920, but ship repairing was carried on until 1936.

The concrete Roman Catholic church on the Bull Bay road looks more like an aeroplane hangar than a church but is hailed by some experts as a 'functional church, original enough to be exciting'. Designed by an Italian, and said to be modelled on the plan of an upturned boat, it is certainly unique and, if not to everyone's taste, is worth seeing.

Bull Bay (Porth Llechog), a mile west of Amlwch, is a sheltered, rocky cove which was formerly a pilot station, and had a thriving ship-building and fishing port in the early 19th century. There is a fine natural rock arch at Porthwen Bay, two miles to the west.

Amlwch lost its branch railway line under the 'rationalization' of railways, but that has not prevented its development as the Anglesey Marine Terminal. Having a special love for the harbour, it was with some trepidation that I re-visited Amlwch Port in 1977, soon after the opening of the Terminal, to see what havoc had been created. I was delighted to find the old harbour little affected by an extension to the quay and the replacement of the old boat house. All the pipes have been laid undergound and great efforts have been made to minimise any disruption of the landscape.

Construction began in 1973 and one of the most modern Signal Buoy moorings in the world has been installed off-shore, with submarine pipe-lines to a Shore Station and twin pipe-lines from Amlwch Port to a transit storage installation at Rhosgoch, two miles inland, connecting with a buried pipe-line 3ft. in diameter laid across Anglesey, the Strait and the mainland of North Wales to the Shell refinery in Cheshire, 78 miles away. Tankers of more than 500,000 tons deadweight can discharge their cargoes of crude oil at the Terminal.

BEAUMARIS. The delightful little town of Beaumaris, at the eastern end of Menai Strait, was for centuries the

County town and the only Municipal Borough in Anglesey, and was the assize town until 1971.

Beaumaris is so compact that the castle and other ancient buildings can be reached with ease, and its attractiveness is enhanced by its unconventional 'promenade' - a wide expanse of turf looking across the shining waters of the Strait to the magnificent panorama of Snowdonia, ever-fascinating and everchanging as sunshine and cloud shadows alternate.

Long before Edward I laid out the town in 1294, and named it 'Bellus Mariscu', which in the Norman -French of his day meant 'the beautiful marsh', the area had been of importance under its Welsh name of Llanfaes. Set at the head of a ferry to the mainland, it was inhabited at least as early as the Bronze Age. The Princes of Gwynedd had one of their residences there; St. Seiriol converted the people to Christianity in the 6th century, and Llywelyn the Great founded Llanfaes in 1237 over the tomb of his wife, Princess Joan, daughter of King John of England.

Edward I removed the Welsh inhabitants of Llanfaes to Rhosyr, in the west of Anglesey, which he renamed Newborough. He replaced them with Englishmen and gave both towns a charter. A year later he began building Beaumaris castle which, although smaller than Caernarfon or Harlech, is the most perfect example of the concentrically planned castles of Great Britain. Dr. Johnson thought the castle 'a mighty pile', adding 'This Castle corresponds with all the representations of romancing narratives. Here is not wanting the private passage, the dark cavity, the deep dungeon, or the lofty tower . . . This is the most compleat view I have yet had of an old Castle. It had a moat.'

Beaumaris castle is still almost surrounded by a moat. It cost £7,000 to build - the equivalent of over £700,000 to-day - and gave employment to '. . . 400 skilled masons, 30 smiths and carpenters, 2,000 unskilled workers and 100 carts and wagons and 30 boats'. During its busiest period the number employed equalled 13 or 14 per cent.

of the workmen in all the trades and commerce of London.

The castle survived an attack by Owain Glyndŵr in 1403, was subsequently captured by him but was retaken in 1405. It was fully defended in the Civil War, when Beaumaris was largely royalist, but surrendered to General Mytton after a battle on the field now known as Cae Brics. In 1660 Robert, Viscount Bulkeley of Baron Hill, claimed that his father had spent over £3,000 in repairs to the castle but by 1785 all the lead and timber and some of the stone had been taken away. Despite this, it remained one of the finest and most complete of the Edwardian castles. It was the scene of a famous Welsh National Eisteddfod in 1832 which was attended by Princess Victoria and her mother, the Duchess of Kent. The castle was handed over to the Office of Works (predecessors of the Department of the Environment) by Sir Richard Williams-Bulkeley, and is now carefully maintained.

Beaumaris did not become a walled town until after the destruction wrought by Owain Glyndŵr. There were three gates and the wall ran along the line of Steeple Lane, which was then the town ditch, to the top of Church Street and from there along the line of Rating Row. Nothing now remains of this wall.

After the Welsh Tudors ascended the English throne Beaumaris enjoyed a Golden Age, trading to foreign ports until its merchants became famous and wealthy, and its houses and inns grew larger and more numerous.

Among the old buildings surviving are The Tudor Rose, 32 Castle Street, dating from 1400, one of the oldest domestic buildings in Anglesey. It was restored during this century to its original condition. Ye Olde Bull's Head (Yr Hen Ben Tarw), also in Castle Street, was originally built in 1472 and rebuilt in 1617. It provided accommodation for the judges of the Assize, and was an important post-house for travellers entering Anglesey via the Llanfaes Ferry. It was commandeered by Mytton when he besieged the castle and now houses many antiques, including the local ducking stool and a water-clock. The stage coach entrance to the courtyard is claimed to have the largest single-hinged door in the British Isles. Both Dr. Johnson and Charles Dickens stayed at the Bull's Head and in 1812 the great Nonconformist preacher, John Elias, sought refuge in it from rioters.

The George and Dragon Hotel in Church Street dates from 1595. It incorporates an older wattle and daub building and has a projecting Tudor upper storey. Some of the old beams and panels remain and an old settle depicts the story of St. George and the Dragon.

The Old David Hughes Grammar School, northwest of the castle, was built in 1603 and endowed by David Hughes, a local benefactor, whose grave is in the parish church. He intended it to provide the youth of Anglesey with a sound classical education, which it did for many years, but it is now a Community Centre. The old Court House, opposite the castle, was built in 1614. The last full Assize Court was held there in 1971. It is now used by the monthly magistrates' Court and is open free at other times. The interior of the Court is paved with flagstones, and massive iron bars separate the paved area from the witness and jury boxes.

The church dates from the early 14th century but the chancel was rebuilt about 1500. It has some fragments of early 16th century stained glass, carved misericordes and several monuments removed from Llanfaes Friary at the Dissolution.

An alabaster table-tomb with the recumbent effigies of an armoured knight and his lady is probably that of a Constable of the castle and his wife. A tablet commemorates members of the Sidney family, ancestors of Sir Philip Sidney. Beatrice Herbert, daughter of the famous Lord Herbert of Cherbury, is buried in the vestry but there is no inscription to her memory. There is a monument by Westmacott to the last Lord Bulkeley, who died in 1822. A mural on the north wall of the south chapel has a 17th century inscription extolling the virtues of 'Margaret, the truly loving wife of Owen Hughes of Beaumaris, Esqr,' traces her distinguished ancestry, and ends 'If you would known more of her, Read the 31st Chapter of Proverbs.'

The 13th century stone sarcophagus of Princess Joan, which was at one time used as a horses' drinking trough, is now preserved in the south porch of the church. There is also a panelled Watchman's Box, formerly in the churchyard, which was used in the early 19th century to guard against bodysnatchers.

Two handsome brasses in the church, one of which is to Richard Bulkeley, c. 1530, an ancestor of the Baron Hill family, now have a warning notice that rubbings are not allowed.

After the Industrial Revolution and with the coming of railways the nearest railway station was at Menai Bridge, and Beaumaris lost its maritime prosperity and developed into a watering-place. It had the wisdom to call in the then well-known architect, Joseph Hansom (inventor of the hansom cab), as adviser. The Bulkeley Arms Hotel, overlooking The Green and the Menai Strait on one side and opening on to Castle Street on the other, the block of buildings known as Victoria Terrace and possibly some of the other fine houses were designed by Hansom.

The Old Gaol, built in 1829 and carefully restored in 1977, is hidden behind intimidatingly high walls. Its wooden treadmill was the last to be used in Britain and is claimed to be the only one in its original position. The cells, including that of the condemned man, with the passage along which he walked to the scaffold, the punishment cells, the work rooms and the exercise yards are on view, together with an exhibition of documents illustrating prison life in the 19th century. There is no better place in which to realise the harsh treatment then meted out to prisoners. The last public execution there was in 1862 when Richard Rowlands was hanged for murder, although protesting his innocence and cursing the church clock facing the scaffold. Despite many attempts at repair, that side of the clock still fails to function satisfactorily.

The Town Hall was rebuilt in 1808 on the site of the original 16th century Town Hall.

Beating the Bounds has been observed in Beaumaris every seven years since the original Charter of Edward I in 1294. Another custom, observed annually, was the 'Hot Coppers' of the Anglesey Hunt, the records of which go back to 1744. At the end of the opening day's hunting the hunters rode in procession around the town, preceded by a brass band, to the Bulkeley Arms Hotel where the chef, attended by the Lady Patroness, scattered hot coins from the balcony to the waiting crowd below. Tradition dictated that the coppers should be £3 in value, but this custom has been discontinued owing to increasing traffic congestion.

Among the much-needed small, unobtrusive light industries attracted to Beaumaris in recent years is the little factory where Anglesey fudge is made.

Just above the town are the ruins of Baron Hill, in a now neglected park. The first house was built by Sir Richard Bulkeley in 1618. Dr. Johnson, who visited it in 1774 thought Lord Bulkeley's house 'very mean' although he admired the grounds. Thomas Pennant, who visited the house in 1776, tells us in his *Tours in Wales* 'The present seat has of late been wholly altered, with excellent taste, by its noble owner, by the advice of that elegant architect Mr. Samuel Wyat.' It was the chief seat of the Bulkeley family, one of the most powerful families in North Wales, who had first settled in Anglesey before 1450 and whose subsidiary branches occupied many of the mansions of Anglesey by the 18th century.

The Sir Richard who built Baron Hill was head of the family from 1572 to 1621. He was a favourite of Elizabeth I and a bitter opponent of the schemes of the Earl of

Leicester in Wales. Later Bulkeleys played a leading part in the island's affairs and in politics, representing in their own person, or through their nominees, both counties and boroughs of Anglesey and Caernarfonshire from the mid-16th to the mid-19th century. The Sir Richard who fought for King Charles during the Civil War was created a Viscount. The peerage became extinct in 1822, and the long line of the Bulkeleys of Baron Hill, which had lasted in unbroken succession for nearly four centuries, was ended. Ownership passed to Sir Richard Williams, son of Lord Bulkeley's halfbrother, who received royal permission to assume the name of Williams-Bulkeley.

The Bulkeley memorial, an obelisk in a field a mile north-west, was raised in 1875. It is on the highest point in the wooded grounds of Baron Hill, and commands superb views.

A mile north of Beaumaris, but within the area of the Borough, is Llanfaes. Between the two is the site of the Franciscan Friary built by Llywelyn the Great, destroyed in 1400 by Henry IV's army and later re-established. It fell into complete ruin after the Dissolution. The site is now owned by Laird (Anglesey) Ltd. in whose factory work was done on Catalina Flying Boats during the 1939-45 war.

Several famous Welsh preachers, including John Elias, John Williams and Llywelyn Lloyd were buried in St. Catherine's church, which was rebuilt in 1845. It is one of the few Anglesey churches with a tall spire. A plate on the wall commemorates the Hamptons of the neighbouring Henllys Hall (now an hotel) from 1460 to 1946. Owen Owen and his two sisters, all three of whom were drowned in the wreck of the *Rothesay Castle* in 1831, are also buried there. Near the church is a simple, long, low building which was the old smithy. In the neighbourhood is Tre Castell, once a residence of the Tudors, but now a farm. The cellars were used to mature metheglin, the mead which was a favourite drink of Elizabeth I.

BENLLECH has grown up in modern times above the two-mile stretch of sands in Benllech Bay on the south-east coast of Anglesey and now reaches almost to Red Wharf Bay. Benllech Bay itself remains unspoilt but houses crowd closely inland. The coastline northwards, with its lofty, rugged cliffs, where an exceptional variety of carboniferous fossils can be found, is indented with coves. Traeth Bychan, half-way between Benllech and Moelfre, is where the submarine *Thetis* grounded in 1939, with the loss of 99 lives. It was later raised and refitted as H.M.S. *Thunderbolt*, and served in the 1939-45 war.

BODEDERN, a small village in which one of the old toll gates of Telford's Holyhead Road still survives, was for centuries the site of the Courts of Commote. The Magistrate's Court House is now used as the Young Men's Institute. Bodedern once had a woollen industry and still has an old-established Agricultural and Horticultural Show which is held annually. North-east of Bodedern are the remains of the Presaddfed Burial Chamber, the Tre-Iorwerth Woods and the reedy Llyn Llywenan which is the haunt of many birds.

CARREGLEFN, an inland village north of the Llyn Alaw Reservoir, has a much restored medieval church retaining three 18th century brasses. Even the churchyard has been tidied up with macadam paths and concrete curbs. Half a mile to the north is a gabled dove-cot beside the road. On the east is Boderwyd, now a farm, which also dates from the 15th century. It was once the home of the Wynns of Boderwyd whose ancestor, Gweirydd Rhys Goch, flourished about 1170 and is considered to be the father of one of the famous 'Fifteen Tribes of North Wales'. Edward Wynn (1681-1755) had a distinguished career in the Church, and became Chancellor of the diocese of Hereford. He did much to help the poet Goronwy Owen in his early career. At Edward Wynn's death Boderwyd passed to Margaret Owen who was also the heiress of Penrhos. She married Sir John Stanley in 1763 and became the mother of the first Lord Stanley of Alderley.

CEMAIS BAY, on the north-east coast of Anglesey, closely resembles a Cornish fishing village. It was a ship-building centre in the 19th century and the most important harbour along that part of the coast until it was superseded by Amlwch Port. A large area of the cliffs overlooking Cemais Bay on the east is owned by the National Trust, including the impressive Hell's Mouth (Porth Gynfor).

The sturdy old stone quay of Cemais is in strong contrast to the stark lines of the nuclear power station on Wylfa Head, on the west of Cemais Bay. An observation tower outside the boundary of the power station is open to the public. It displays illustrations and information about the Wylfa station. The car park is also a starting point for the hour-long Wylfa Nature Trail around the headland.

Magnificent cliffs extend westward to Carmel Head (Trwyn y Gadair), past Cemlyn Bay which was once a haunt of smugglers and pirates, with the almost inevitable story of hidden treasure. A shallow sea-water lagoon, almost sealed off from the bay by a long, narrow spit of sand, is a bird sanctuary where only the most insensitive visitors will attempt to walk between April and June, when the birds are nesting. The sandspit and the neighbouring headland of Trewin Cemlyn are a Nature Reserve owned by the National Trust.

Cemlyn had an important lifeboat station from 1828 to 1919, which was at one time in the charge of the Rev. Owen Lloyd Williams of Llanrhyddlad, son of the Rev. James Williams and his wife Frances of Llanfair-yng-Nghornwy who did so much for the lifeboat movement in Anglesey. Near the sea on the west of the bay is the church of Llanrhwydrys, reached by a farm track crossing a causeway over the marsh. It was founded in

33

A.D. 570, rebuilt in the 12th century and a larger chancel added in the following century. There is a gallery with a beam dated 1776 and the cruck supporting the chancel roof was left free-standing when the nave wall was demolished to add a north chapel.

DULAS, on the north-west coast of Anglesey, is on an estuary of the Dulas river, opening into an almost land-locked bay, protected by sand-banks covered in sea-lavender and other plants characteristic of sand-dunes. Dulas was a busy place in the 19th century when clay was cut from the low cliffs, lime was burnt in the kilns and fuel for the now deserted brickworks was landed at the quay. Always a dangerous coast for sailing vessels, a tower was set up on Ynys Dulas in 1824 as a landmark and was stored by the lady of the manor with food and drink for any shipwrecked sailors who were stranded there. The little island is a haunt of grey seals.

A granite Celtic cross standing on a low mound beside the A.5025 road was set up in 1910 by the Honourable Society of Cymmrodorion, the oldest of the London-Welsh Societies. It commemorates the Morris brothers of Llanfihangel Tre'r-beirdd who grew up in a farm overlooking Dulas Bay.

The ruins of the medieval church of Llanwenllwyfo are hidden in the woods of Llysdulas House, north of the Bay. Llanwenllwyfo village, now by-passed by the new road to Amlwch, has a new church, with a narrow spire, set on high ground beside the lane running down to the sandy shore. It is well worth a visit in spite of its unpromising exterior. It has an old font, an oak screen, a brass of 1609 commemorating Marcelie Lloyd and family of Llysdulas, brought from the old church and 11 windows of very fine 15th and 16th century Flemish glass, depicting townscapes, landscapes and tiled interiors, with figures, probably brought from France by a former owner of Llysdulas.

It was off this coast that one of the largest

concentrations of ships was assembled in 1944, in readiness for D Day.

HOLYHEAD (Caer Gybi) is by far the largest town of Anglesey and has been a port for Ireland, and of major importance for its position on one of the great traffic routes of Western Europe, since the dawn of recorded history. Its fine parish church is protected by the well-preserved walls of a 3rd century Roman fortification and a small coastguard fort lies beneath the churchyard which is on low cliffs, then washed by the sea, but since reclaimed.

Packet boats were in operation between Holyhead and Dublin in 1575 and the mail service was never interrupted, even during the two world wars, until 23 May, 1970, when fire damaged the Tubular railway bridge over the Menai Strait and the mail had to be diverted to Heysham until repairs to the bridge were completed. The first train to run across the bridge after the fire was greeted with civic rejoicings on arrival at Holyhead on 30 January, 1972.

In the days of sail there were numerous inns, for intending passengers could sometimes be detained in Holyhead for days, or even weeks, awaiting a favourable wind. The letters and diaries of 18th century travellers were full of complaints about the boredom of the delays.

The choice of Holyhead as the terminus of Telford's great road from London in 1815 brought great changes. By 1821 the *Cambrian Tourist* reported that Holyhead had changed '. . . from a poor fishing village to a decent looking town in consequence of its being the chief resort of passengers to and from Dublin', and that in addition to the sailing packets, 'government has, this year, placed steam packets on this station . . . The passage will be effected in from five and a half to seven hours . . .' Holyhead became a rail terminus in 1849, although Stephenson's tubular bridge over the Menai Strait was not completed until 1850.

35

Holyhead has one of the oldest surviving docks in the kingdom, with a pumping station installed in 1820. The Custom House dates from 1850 and there is a Doric memorial arch to commemorate the visit of George IV in 1821. It also marks the end of the A.5 road. The Inner Harbour, with its docks, quays and warehouses, was constructed in 1875 and is overlooked by an obelisk commemorating Capt. Skinner, who was foremost in promoting the harbour improvements. He was drowned in 1832, in the wreck of his packet ship, so ironically named *Escape*.

Beyond the Harbour is the open sea, with an upper and lower promenade skirting Newry Beach. Another promenade extends for a mile and a half along the breakwater which commands wide views of the coast and the Skerries. The lighthouse at the end of the breakwater was last manned in 1962 but still has its brass Victorian clock-work machinery. Salt Island (Ynys Halen) on the east of the harbour is not an island at all. It derives its name from an 18th century factory for extracting salt from sea-water.

Holyhead is now being developed technologically on a large scale. The multi-purpose British Rail Ferry, *St. Columba*, went into service on 2 May, 1977, carrying rail passengers, motorists and their cars, and commercial road vehicles. There is also a special ferry for ships carrying aluminium for the Anglesey Aluminium Smelter, and a modern purpose-built container service. Although Holyhead is so far from any great city centre the port is so important in European eyes that the E.E.C. gave a grant of £500,000 towards a new industrial estate for 'port-related' industries.

The comfortable berths on the ferries and the passage of only three to three and a half hours to or from Dublin has resulted in the closing down of most of the hotels of mail coach and sailing days. Even the railway hotel is shut, and may be demolished, as passengers rush by train or car from the harbour and miss all that Holyhead and its surroundings can offer.

The parish church of St. Cybi, just off the steep, winding main street, near the town centre, is on the site of the 6th century church founded by the saint. The earliest part now dates from the 13th century, and the nave and transepts from the 15th to the 16th century. It was considerably restored in the Victorian era and the organ was brought from the library of Eaton Hall. A chapel added in 1897 contains a life-size effigy of the Hon. R.C. Stanley of Penrhos who carried out much antiquarian research in the latter half of the 19th century. The chapel also has some fine 19th century stained glass by Sir Edward Burne-Jones and William Morris. The exterior of St. Cybi's is very striking, with an elaborate porch, bands of quatrefoil ornament, and battlements decorated with coats of arms and small animals, including dragons.

The much smaller Capel Eglwys-y-Bedd (Church of the Grave) nearby is all that remains of a medieval church which reputedly contains the grave of Seregri, leader of a band of Irish invaders expelled from Anglesey.

HOLY ISLAND. None of the earlier travellers showed the slightest interest in the magnificent cliff scenery of Holy Island or in its prehistoric remains. It was George Borrow who led the way in appreciation of the sense of the past which broods over Holy Island and the poetry which is in the very air.

Holy Island is joined to mainland Anglesey only by the Stanley Embankment, carrying the A.5 and the railway line, and by the Four Mile Bridge carrying the B.454 Valley-Trearddur-Holyhead road, although Holy Island is almost joined to the mainland at low tide.

Holyhead Mountain (Mynydd Twr) rises to a height of just over 700ft. west of Holyhead. On a clear day the whole of Anglesey, the mountains of Mourne, the Isle of Man and Snowdonia can be seen from the summit.

A signal station was set up on Holyhead Mountain in 1810 as the first of a chain of stations to bring news of shipping to Liverpool owners and mechants in the days of tea and wheat races. At its trial it was claimed that a signal was transmitted in 1 minute, but 5 to 6 minutes was more usual. Other stations in the chain were on Point Lynas, Puffin Island, the Great Orme, Llysfaen and Point of Ayr to Chester and Liverpool.

The remains of Caer-y-Twr, the fortress on the summit from which the mountain derives its Welsh name, covers 17 acres.

The heathery slopes are thickly strewn with prehistoric remains. The Cytiau'r Gwyddelod (Irishmen's Huts), some of which have walls as much as 2 ft. high, hearths and beds, were occupied by skilled woodsmen and metal workers who always had the closest possible contact with Ireland, although doubt has been thrown upon the possibility that they were Irishmen. They traded in axes, gold and other goods. Also on Holy Island are the sites of the oratories of numerous Celtic saints.

The great cliffs of Gogarth Bay, between North and South Stacks, are a popular training ground for rock climbers and are riddled with great caverns haunted by huge colonies of birds. The birds and their eggs are stringently protected by legislation, as in foggy weather their raucous cries give shipping warning of the dangerous rocks. July is the best month to see the myriads of young birds and hear the amazing noise they make. Grey seals breed in caves at the foot of the cliffs and can sometimes be seen swimming. The South Stack can be reached by boat, or by a road to the automated lighthouse which was built in 1808. There are steep steps down the cliffs and a short suspension bridge to South Stack.

Ellin's Tower, a small castellated building on the edge of the cliff, was built in the 19th century by one of the Stanleys of Alderley as a summer house. The cliff tops between the Tower and the lighthouse have been leased to the Royal Society for the Protection of Birds as a bird sanctuary, and a Nature Trail borders the 350 steps to the lighthouse.

Penrhos House, south-east of Holyhead, has been partly demolished. It was the home of the Stanleys of Alderley. The estate was bought by the Anglesey Aluminium Company in 1968 and there is now a giant smelter south of the A.5, but north of the highway, on Penrhos Head, is a Nature Reserve covering 45 acres and a breeding site for sea and wading birds, to which access is restricted. A two-mile long Nature Trail begins near the Toll House on the Stanley Embankment.

LLANALLGO. The 15th century church of Llanallgo has an inscribed 13th century bell and a small obelisk in the churchyard commemorating the wreck of the *Royal Charter* off the coast at Moelfre in 1859. Dickens, in *The Uncommercial Traveller*, pays tribute to the Rev. Stephen Hughes and his family for their unremitting efforts to identify the bodies of the 452 people who were drowned in the disaster, and to comfort the grief-stricken relatives.

Farther south is the Parciau plateau which was the scene of a great battle between the Danes and the Welsh in A.D. 872. There are remnants of a prehistoric fortress in the woods of the Parciau estate; also a 17th century dove-cot and the restored 12th century Llaneugrad church, with a 16th century transept and a roughly carved 13th century crucifix with an arresting, agonized figure of Christ.

LLANBABO. Part of the agricultural parish of Llanbabo was submerged when the Llyn Alaw Reservoir was built but the little medieval church remains, beside a stream crossed by a stone bridge. It has an incised 14th century carving, believed to represent St. Pabo, an early 6th century chieftain, shown as a crowned king with his sceptre.

LLANBADRIG. The church is on a headland east of

Cemais Bay. It is on one of the oldest church sites in Anglesey and is the only ancient church on the island dedicated to St. Patrick, who is said to have founded it as a thank offering for his survival from a shipwreck on Middle Mouse Island. A 10th century sepulchral slab has a crudely incised vertical decoration of unusual design.

The church is reached by a farm road and its very plain exterior gives little hint of the mosque-like interior, which is due to the 3rd Lord Stanley of Alderley who made it a condition of his donation towards the restoration that it should be in the Islamic style. This eccentric uncle of Bertrand Russell had become a Moslem, and among other strange stories told of him is that he married the same Spanish lady four times - twice by Mahommedan, and once each by Roman Catholic and Civil rites - only to find all four were invalid as the lady already had a husband!

East of Llanbadrig is Dinas Gynfor, the most northerly point of Wales, which divides Porth Llanlleiana from Porth Gynfor (Hell's Mouth). Four and a half acres of the cliffland belong to the National Trust, including the Iron Age promontory fort, somewhat damaged by quarrying, which covers an area of 700 by 500 yards, and is defended by cliffs dropping 200 ft. sheer to the sea and a marsh on the landward side.

LLANDDANIEL, south-west of Menai Bridge, has some of the loveliest reaches of the Menai Strait and many prehistoric burial mounds, of which the finest is the Neolithic Bryn Celli Ddu (The Mound of the Dark Grove). An authoritative booklet by Frances Lynch, issued by the Department of the Environment, describes the two religious monuments - a passage grave and a henge - which make it a very rare instance of direct contact between two religious traditions. The henge, with its circle of upright stones, was built over, soon after erection, by adherents of an older tradition who built a large passage grave and cairn. Both monuments can be traced clearly. The burial chamber is reached through a 20 ft. passage. It has a replica of the original central pillar stone, with its interesting incised pattern, which is now in the National Museum of Wales at Cardiff.

Plas Newydd, the family home of the Marquesses of Anglesey and their ancestors for five centuries, was given to the National Trust in 1976 with 169 acres of land and one and a half miles of the Menai coastline. The seventh Marquess, who is a military historian, still lives there with the Marchioness, who is a daughter of the novelist Charles Morgan and his wife, Hilda Vaughan, a native of Builth, Breconshire, who wrote novels steeped in the Welsh atmosphere of that county.

Plas Newydd was rebuilt to the designs of James Wyatt in the late 18th and early 19th centuries and was extensively altered in the 1930's when Rex Whistler, a friend of the family, painted his famous mural. It is the largest and finest of those he completed before his too early death. The house has fine furniture, paintings and an exhibition of Rex Whistler's work.

The small military museum displays campaign relics collected by the first Marquess, then Lord Uxbridge. It includes the 'Anglesey leg' which he used to replace the leg shot off at Waterloo. It was one of the first articulated limbs ever made.

The house and grounds command magnificent views of the Strait and Snowdonia, and the woods have oaks, sycamores and pine trees of enormous size. Among the interesting shrubs in the garden is a giant plant of *Rhododendron Mollyanum*, planted in the 1930's. By 1977 it measured over 30 ft. in diameter and about 20 ft. in height.

Llanedwen church, rebuilt in 1856, is inside the walls of the Plas Newydd grounds. It has interesting 15th and 17th century carvings incorporated in the pulpit and is the burial place of Henry Rowlands, of Plas Gwyn, author of *Mona Antiqua Restaurata*, highly valued by his contemporaries. Although many of his theories have proved incorrect, as a pioneer in this field he deserves credit for preserving the history of a number of places which would otherwise have been unknown to us in the present day.

A field in the parish is still called 'Maes Mawr y Gad' (Field of the Great Army). It is said to be the place where the Romans destroyed the Druids after crossing the Moel y Don Ferry from Caernarfonshire, although others think they made the crossing by the Aber Menai Ferry. Plas Coch, a Tudor mansion which was the home of the Hughes family, is now the centre of a caravan site, complete with barbecue and discotheque.

LLANDDEUSANT, an inland parish in the north-west of Anglesey, has two famous mills. The 18th century Llynon Windmill has three pairs of millstones, hoists for lifting and lowering grain, and a device for warning when the hoppers are almost empty. The small but attractive Howell Watermill has an overshot wheel and has been in use for 600 years. The church was built in 1861 by an amateur architect who 'shrinks from the public gaze' - as well he might have done!

On Glan Alaw Farm, south-west of Llyn Alaw, is Bedd Branwen, the traditional burial place of the ill-fated heroine of *The Mabinogion* story of *Branwen, Daughter of Llŷr*, for whom 'a four-sided grave was made . . . and she was buried on the bank of the Alaw'.

Sir William Williams, Speaker of the House of Commons in the reign of Charles II, was born at Nantanog in the neighbouring parish of Llantrisant.

LLANEILIAN, on the north-east coast, has a 15th century church of exceptional interest, with a 12th century pepper-box tower, a curious little chapel approached by a passage, and a splendidly carved rood-screen and loft. There is a painting of a skeleton on the rood-loft and the inscription 'Colyn Angau yw Pechod' (The sting of death is sin). There are also carved and painted corbels depicting musicians playing flutes and bagpipes, and 16th to 17th century choir-stalls. The little chapel of St. Eilian has a different line of orientation from the main building. It stands on the site of the original foundation which is believed to date from the earliest establishment of Christianity in Anglesey in the 5th century. In the chapel are a fine old chest, a pair of dog-tongs and the wooden base of a panelled shrine. It was believed that those who could squeeze through the space left by a missing panel and turn round without touching the sides would have good fortune, but if they touched the sides they would have bad luck or even die.

Ffynnon Eilian, north-west of the church, beside a small stream, was noted for its health-giving qualities, but fell from grace in the 19th century and became a cursing well.

A lighthouse and a signal and telegraph station were established in 1835 by the Trustees of the Liverpool Docks on Point Lynas, which shelters Port Eilian. Ships en route for Merseyside take on pilots here.

LLANFAIR MATHAFARN EITHAF, north-west of Beaumaris, has a church dating from the 12th or 13th century, but much restored. In the neighbourhood are Pant-y-Saer, a late Neolithic burial chamber on a limestone ridge giving superb views ranging from Great Orme to Snowdonia. An Iron Age hut group, half a mile away, has yielded Romano-British relics. Glyn, an early 17th century farmhouse, has unique plaster decorations and an overmantel panel depicting a potentate sitting under palm trees, receiving ambassadors. A chimney piece is engraved with plants.

The Rev. Goronwy Owen, greatest of the 18th century Welsh poets, was born in the parish in 1723. George Borrow pays eloquent tribute to Goronwy Owen's exquisite verse, which gave new life to Welsh poetry, and visited his birthplace which is generally believed to be Y Dafarn Goch, the family homestead at Brynteg. It is reached down a narrow grassy lane and has been viewed since by admirers from all over the world, although it is not open to the public.

The Village Hall at Brynteg is a memorial to the poet, who overcame all obstacles in his desire for learning but had a life-long struggle with poverty in ill-paid curacies until he emigrated to America in 1758. He was appointed headmaster of the Grammar School attached to the College of William and Mary, Williamstown, Virginia, and taught there until the death of his wife. He was appointed to the living of St. Andrew's, Brunswick County, Virginia, in 1760. He died in 1769 and was buried on a plantation he had bought there. Celebrations were held in Williamstown during his bi-centenary and as a result of a world-wide appeal a new pulpit was given to Llanfair Mathafarn Eithaf church in which he had served for a few months as a curate.

LLANFAIR P.G., or LLANFAIR PWLL, has several claims to fame but is best known for having the longest platform ticket in the world. It gives an extension of its proper name of Llanfair Pwllgwyngyll to Llanfairpwllgwyngyllgogerychwyrndrobwllllandysilio-gogogoch, which probably originated in a 19th century hoax. The English translation is 'St. Mary's church in a hollow by the white hazel close to the rapid whirlpool by the red cave of St. Tysilio.' It it still so far descriptive that the church of St. Mary is in the township and St. Tysilio's church can be found in a deep hollow at the foot of an alarmingly steep lane, by the shores of the Menai Strait where whirlpools created by the tides rise and fall over 20 ft., but the red cave can no longer be found and the white hazels have been replaced by oaks and elms.

It was in Yr Hafoty, Llanfair P.G., that the first Women's Institute in Great Britain was formed on 11 September, 1915, with Welsh and English members, at the suggestion of a Canadian visitor. It has since spread all over the British Isles.

The Toll House at Llanfair P.G. was designed by Telford and still displays its list of charges. The Holyhead Road was under the control of the Turnpike Trust longer than any other in the Kingdom, and the Anglesey gates were not removed until 1 November, 1895.

Tŷ Coch was for many years the home of Sir John Morris-Jones, poet and grammarian and translator of the *Rubá'iát of Omar Khayyám* into Welsh. He was appointed lecturer in Welsh at the University College of North Wales, Bangor, in 1889. Two years later a Chair of Welsh was created for him. This dignified, but genial man devoted his life to the study of the Welsh language and the standardization of its orthography, and was an adjudicator at the National Eisteddfod from 1896 to 1928. His adjudications inaugurated a new period in the history of Welsh literature and letters. He died in 1929. A Celtic cross marks his grave in Llanfair P.G. churchyard.

The Anglesey Column, high above the waters of the Menai Strait, is on a wooded, rocky hill beside the A.5. It commemorates the first Marquess of Anglesey who, as Lord Paget and later Earl of Uxbridge, fought in the Peninsular War and at Waterloo. The column was built of Moelfre marble in 1816 but his statue, in the old Hussar uniform, was not set up on its summit until 1860. The top of the column is reached by 115 steps.

There is another gigantic mid-19th century statue on the sea-weedy shore of the Strait, below the Britannia Bridge, of Admiral Lord Nelson. It was designed by Lord Clarence Paget, the sailor sculptor, as a navigation mark.

The great Britannia Railway Bridge was the first tubular bridge in the world. It was built by Robert Stephenson in the face of much opposition to his ideas but with the encouragement of the great engineer Sir William Fairbairn. The staggering difficulties of bridging the Strait with a structure of sufficient rigidity to enable a train to cross were made still greater by the insistence of the Admiralty that the bridge must be a clear 100 ft.

above high water, and by their refusal to allow any interruption of the passage of shipping during its construction. It took four years to complete and was opened to traffic in 1850. Two hundred years later it was so badly damaged by fire that it had to be closed for two years. It was largely rebuilt, the new structure making provision for a road deck over the track at some future date.

The bridge took its name from a rock on which the central pillar rests. A ship named *Britannia* had been wrecked on the rock a few years previously. There are two colossal lions crouching at each end of the bridge.

LLANFAIR-YNG-NGHORNWY, on the extreme north-west of Anglesey, has a steep rock-bound coast, including many islets, the most important group of which is the Skerries, the ancient Welsh name of which was Ynys Moelrhoniaid (Isle of Porpoises). They are two miles off Carmel Head (Trwyn y Gadair). Before the present lighthouse was built a coal fire in a conical grate was established there in 1716. It was the first lighthouse in the district, built on the initiative of Liverpool merchants and maintained by private individuals who collected a small toll from passing vessels to pay their expenses. Between 80 and 100 tons of coal were burnt there every year. Trinity House made several offers for the light and finally purchased it in 1841. It was the last privately owned lighthouse in the country.

Viking raiders landed on the shingle beach of Fydlyn Cove. Pen Bryn-yr-Eglwys takes its name from the site of a vanished Celtic chapel and there are traces of a cliff fort on the headland. Craig-y-gwynt had one of the stations of the Holyhead-Liverpool telegraph in the 19th century.

The walls of the nave and the chancel arch of the restored parish church date from about 1100, and a south chapel from the 16th century. There is a memorial to Evan Thomas 'a most skilful bonesetter', who died in 1814. He was the ancestor of a distinguished line of bonesetters, the best known of whom was Hugh Owen Thomas, born at Bodedern in 1834. He set up in practice as an orthopaedic surgeon in Liverpool and invented the Thomas Splint, now almost universally used in England and America. Many of his monographs have been incorporated in modern text books. When he died in 1891 his work was comparatively unknown outside Liverpool, but his nephew, Sir Robert Jones, who had joined him at the age of 21 as a professional assistant, carried on his work. He organized military hospitals and centres for orthopaedic treatment in the 1914-18 war, and the present emphasis on rehabilitation grew out of the principles he enunciated.

Another distinguished man buried at Llanfair-yng-Nghornwy is the Rev. James Williams, born in 1790, who was rector of LLanddeusant, Llangaffo and Llanfair-yng-Nghornwy. He was a highly respected 'squarson' of the old school and a zealous supporter of the National Eisteddfod. He was promoted Chancellor of Bangor Cathedral in 1851 and paved the way for (Sir) John Rhys, but he is best remembered for the work he and his wife, Frances, did for the lifeboat movement. Frances founded the Anglesey Association for the Preservation of Life from Shipwreck; together they raised funds to place much needed lifeboats along the dangerous Anglesey coast and in 1835 James was awarded a gold medal for personal bravery in rescue work. It was largely through the efforts of Frances Williams that the first lifeboat station in North Wales was established.

Caerau, north of the church, is an attractive 17th and early 18th century farmhouse approached by a sycamore avenue. The plain exterior gives little hint of its panelled rooms, built-in cupboards and dressers, which are typical of the period.

LLANFECHELL is an inland parish, south of Cemais Bay, with one of the few churches in Anglesey which is actually in the centre of the village it serves. It is of very early foundation, rebuilt in the 12th century, and has fragments of 15th century glass and an Elizabethan chalice. The 16th century tower is topped by a curious beehive-shaped cap.

William Bulkeley was born in the neighbouring manor-house of Brynddu in 1691 and the enduring interest of the house is due to the diaries in which he chronicled the minutest details of his life and expenditure on family, house, garden and home farm. The surviving volumes cover the years 1734 to 1743, and from 1747 to within a month of his death in 1760. Some commentators have called him 'difficult', and it is true he was rather too ready to embark on unjustifiable lawsuits, but any man could be pardoned for being 'difficult' who had his family troubles to contend with, but he was a staunch friend to anyone he liked, including his kinsmen Henry Morgan of Henblas and Prichard Morris, father of the Morris brothers of Llanfihangel Tre'r-beirdd. He had a great love for the land and certainly had a very human and compassionate side to his character. He was widowed early and brought up his extremely unsatisfactory children with considerable kindness and indulgence, only to be landed with a brood of grandchildren resulting from his daughter's far from happy marriage to the famous privateer, Fortunatus Wright.

The Diaries were inherited by Henry Morgan and, together with the Henblas manuscripts, are on loan to the Bangor University Library. They are the basis for Mrs. Nesta Evans's *Life in Eighteenth Century Anglesey*. Extracts from William Bulkeley's own Diaries have been edited by Miss B. Dew Roberts in her fascinating book. It has the rather misleading title *Mr. Bulkeley and the Pirate*, which is more suggestive of a lurid novel than the scholarly work it is.

Double daffodils planted by William Bulkeley in his garden now grow wild and relics of him and his family, including those of Fortunatus Wright, are preserved in the house. His walled garden survives.

Llanfechell is the only village conservation area in Anglesey.

LLANFIHANGEL TRE'R-BEIRDD, east of Llannerchymedd, is a parish in which some of the most remarkable natives of Anglesey were born. William Jones (1675?-1749), a distinguished mathematician, was born at Merddyn. He was a friend of Halley and Newton, some of whose works he edited, and became Vice-President of the Royal Society. His son, Sir William Jones (1746-1794), won great fame as a philologist and was an authority on Hindu law.

Tyddyn Melus, the next small farm to Merddyn, was the birthplace of Morris Prichard (Morys ap·Rhisiart), 1674-1763, who married Margaret Owen of Bodafon y glyn, a neighbouring farm. They were the parents of the famous 'Morrisiaid Môn'. He is buried in the churchyard of Llanfihangel Tre'r-beirdd.

The eldest son, Lewis (Llewelyn Ddu o Fôn), a poet and scholar, was also born at Tyddyn Melus, in 1701. He held an official position as 'waiter and searcher' at the Custom House in Beaumaris and Holyhead and was employed by the Navy Office to make a survey of Welsh Ports. His invaluable *Plans of Harbours, Bays and Roads in St. George's and the Bristol Channels* was published in 1801. He was succeeded as 'waiter and searcher' at Holyhead by Owen Davies, who had married Lewis's sister, Ellen Morris.

The family moved to Y Fferem, in the same parish, where Richard, founder of the influential London-Welsh Society, the Hon. Society of Cymmrodorion, William, botanist, antiquary and letter-writer, and John, who became a sailor and died in 1740 during the unsuccessful attack on Cartagena, were born. A final move was made to Pentrerianell in 1707.

The letters of the Morris brothers to each other and to their friends are a mine of information about Welsh and London-Welsh affairs. George Borrow, who was a great admirer of the brothers, has much to say about them in *Wild Wales* although, as he did not have access to the vast amount of documentation we have today, some of his details are not quite correct.

The church of Llanfihangel Tre'r-beirdd has been completely rebuilt but has numerous wall monuments and other relics of the earlier church. There is a large maen-hir south of the church and the parish includes part of Mynydd Bodafon, a low hill with several small lakes, and the prehistoric Cytiau'r Gwyddelod.

LLANGADWALADR, on the A.4080 road to Aberffraw, is reputedly the burial place of Welsh princes. The Early English church, dedicated to St. Cadwaladr, is said to have been founded by the saintly king himself. He is portrayed in his royal robes in some of the finest stained glass in Anglesey, re-set in the 15th century east window. An early 7th century stone, now in the church, describes his grandfather, Cadfan, King of Gwynedd, as 'the wisest and most illustrious of kings'.

South of the little village is Bodorgan, home of the Meyrick family from Tudor times but rebuilt in 1800. The woods reach down to the north shore of the Malltraeth estuary of the Cefni river, looking across to the National Nature Reserve of Newborough Forest on the other side of the estuary. Owen Meyrick, M.P. for Anglesey from 1715 to 1722, was of considerable assistance to Lewis Morris and his brothers in their careers.

On the same estate, but nearer the estuary, is all that remains of Bodowen (or Bodeon), the home of the Owen family which came to prominence in the reign of Elizabeth I and at one time had a close political affinity with the Meyricks. The first Sir Hugh Owen married the heiress of Orielton in Pembrokeshire. The two branches of the family contrived not to get involved on either side in the Civil War, although the classical memorial to Col. Hugh Owen in the Owen Chapel of Llangadwaladr church, erected by his wife Ann in 1660, gives the impression that he was a gallant royalist.

LLANGEFNI, approximately in the centre of Anglesey, is now the administrative capital. It is on the banks of the Afon Cefni, which was navigable up to the town until 1760. Those who imagine that Anglesey is bleak and flat are pleasantly surprised by the steep hill down into the town from Telford's old Holyhead road and the beautiful woods in the neighbourhood. There is a delightful riverside path through the wooded valley, past two weirs which once provided water storage for a mill downstream. The attractive parish church, St. Cyngar's, was rebuilt in 1824 but has a 5th century inscribed gravestone and a 12th century front.

Tregarnedd, a private house on the outskirts of the town, has a mound marking the site of a castle of Ednyfed Fychan, counsellor of Llywelyn the Great and ancestor of the Tudor dynasty.

Llangefni was the scene of the labours of two of the greatest Welsh Nonconformist preachers, Christmas Evans and John Elias. Christmas Evans had charge of the Baptist congregations in Anglesey from 1791 to 1826, when they were regarded as branches of one church. He was chiefly associated with the chapel at Cildwrn, a mile or so out of the town.

John Elias was one of those chosen for full ministerial work among the Calvinistic Methodists in North Wales after the break from the Established Church. He made an immense impression with his great personal dignity and conviction and his electrifying oratory. The latter part of his life was spent at Fron, near Llangefni, where he died in 1841. He played a prominent part in the drawing up of the Confession of Faith in 1823 and the Constitutional Deed in 1826. Capel Dinas, in which he ministered in Llangefni, no longer exists.

A ring of stones marking the site of Gorsedd ceremonies during the National Eisteddfod of Wales in 1957 holds special memories for me as it was there I was admitted into the Gorsedd as an Honorary bard by the then Archdruid, Wil Ifan.

LLANGEINWEN, at the southern end of the Menai Strait, was formerly linked more closely with Caernarfon, a mile away across the water, by the Foel Ferry than with Anglesey towns. Caernarfon was then the market town of the parish but since the Ferry closed it is 17 miles away by road.

It is a well-wooded area, bounded on the north and west by the Afon Braint, with the long narrow estuary separating it from Newborough Warren. Mud-flats, which are a haunt of herons and oyster-catchers, are exposed at low tide.

The 12th century church is on an early site. It was carefully restored between the two world wars under the supervision of Harold Hughes of Bangor, an authority on ancient churches. It has a carved 13th century font, 9th and 11th century carved grave slabs re-set in the tower buttresses, a 19th century brass chandelier and pews, and an 18th century memorial to Margaret Williams '. . . whose remains are deposited beneath in hopes of resuming the same At the general Ressurection' (sic). A mural commemorates the death by drowning in 1941 of Sir David Owen, General Manager of the Port of London Authority, on his return from a Mission in Hong Kong to advise on the future of the port there.

The lonely little church of Llanfair-y-cymwd, a mile away, is reached by a grassy lane bounded by high stone walls and hedges and shaded with trees.

The B.44219 to the Ferry runs for the last mile right on the brink of the water to the Mermaid Inn, which was burnt down but was being rebuilt in the same style when I was last there, early in 1977. There are wonderful views of Snowdonia and the Peninsula of Lleyn, with the Strait looking more like a land-locked lake than dangerous tidal waters.

In the early 19th century both the Foel and the Aber Menai ferry boats sank in the same year, the only survivor on both occasions being the same man, Hugh Williams of Bodowr!

LlANGRISTIOLUS. St. Christiolus church, south of a cross-roads of the A.5, was re-constructed in the 12th century and well restored in 1852. The chancel is wider than the nave, from which it is separated by an arch which adds to a sense of spaciousness.

Henblas, the old home of the Morgans, has a round Gothic entrance lodge, untypical of Anglesey, on the B.4422. Henry Morgan of Henblas was the 'Cousin Morgan' referred to in the diaries of William Bulkeley of Brynddu, Llanfechell, which, together with the household accounts of Henblas, are one of the chief sources of information about 18th century Anglesey.

Just beyond the lodge of Henblas are the remains of the enormous Henblas barn. The date 1776 and a lion rampant decorate one of the arches over the great doorways.

LlANGWYLLOG marks the centre of Anglesey. The church of St. Cwyllog is reached by a farm track branching off on the west of the B.5111 road from Llangefni to Llannerchymedd. The attractive site is in a hollow beside a stream. The church has 16th century windows and doors, 18th century pulpit, pews and communion rails, with a reading desk dated 1769. There are also some good memorials and a 13th century tub font carved with a leaf pattern and cable moulding.

LlANIDEN is a peaceful, well-wooded parish running down to the shore of the Menai Strait. Among the pre-historic sites in the parish are the scanty remains of Castell Idris, a British fort; Caer Leb, 200 ft. by 160 ft., a fort which was occupied in the 3rd century A.D., and the Bodowyr cromlech burial chamber above the marshy bank of the Afon Braint.

Llaniden Old Church, founded by St. Niden about

616, is romantically situated in a belt of trees beside Llaniden House, with cowslips, primroses and wild orchis decorating the roadside between Brynsiencyn and the church in Spring. The church is close to the Strait but the view is hidden by woods. St. Niden's is now dank and desolate, with its almost circular churchyard overgrown with wild garlic and all its fittings removed to the new church built at Brynsiencyn in 1843. St. Niden's was at one time an off-shoot of the Augustinian Priory of Beddgelert, Caernarfonshire, and became the parish church after the Dissolution. Most of the church was demolished, but an arcade remains, detached, in the churchyard. The old Holy well of St. Niden is in the grounds of Plas Llaniden. Water in a stoup of the church is said always to maintain the same level, and Giraldus Cambrensis tells of Y Maen Morddwyd, a miraculous thigh bone which, it was said, would always return to the church if taken away but which cannot now be found. The Rev. Henry Rowlands of Plas Gwyn, author of *Mona Antiqua*, was given the living of Llaniden in 1696.

LLANIESTYN. The simple little 14th century church of St. Iestyn has a porch dated about 1510 and a remarkable stone carving in low relief showing St. Iestyn in a hermit's robe. His long moustache, drooping over a conventionally treated beard, gives him a melancholy look, but it is a superb example of 14th century work.

The restored 15th century church of Llanfihangel Din Sylwy (St. Michael's), a mile to the north, has a well-carved 17th century wooden pulpit. The church is sheltered by the great prehistoric hill-fort of Din Sylwy (also known as Bwrdd Arthur) on a magnificent site overlooking Red Wharf Bay and commanding a view of the coast from Port Lynas in north-east Anglesey to Great Orme in Caernarfonshire. The stone-lined rampart encloses about 17 acres, with traces of hut circles which formed the largest British camp in Anglesey. It dates from the 1st to the 4th century A.D., and possibly earlier.

Pottery and Roman coins have been found there.

LLANNERCH-Y-MEDD, set where the B.5112 meets the B.5111, has a market established in 1657 which was the largest in Anglesey until the Llangefni market was opened. The Farmers' Club was founded in 1843.

Llannerchymedd still claims to be 'the hub of rural Anglesey' but, apart from market days, it is considerably more peaceful than it was in the mid-19th century when there were 250 bootmakers employed there and printers, snuff, clog and clock makers also flourished.

East of Llannerchymedd, on the road to Red Wharf Bay, is Clorach where St. Cybi and St. Seiriol used to meet each other, but the famous holy wells no longer exist. As those who still read Matthew Arnold's poetry know, his poem *East and West* describes how St. Cybi, who journeyed from and to Holyhead, always faced the sun and became so sunburnt that he was known as 'Cybi the Dark', whilst St. Seiriol, travelling from and to Penmon, had his back to the sun, and was known as 'Seiriol the Fair'.

LLANSADWRN, west of Beaumaris, has one of the oldest stone memorials in Wales, inscribed to Saturnius and his saintly wife, and believed by Nash-Williams to date from A.D. 530. Saturnius has been identified with Sadwrn Farchog, the founder of the church, who was a brother of St. Illtyd. Primroses grow thickly on either side of the path to the church, which has a double bell-cot. In spite of no less than five restorations in the 19th century, there are several memorials including one to John Davies, who died in 1825 aged 88, which says he 'blended the active discharge of every social duty with a liberality of sentiment, a piety and a cheerfulness rarely united'.

Sir Andrew Crombie Ramsey (1814-91), President of the Royal Geological Society and pioneer of North Wales geology, is buried in the churchyard and his grave is marked by a glacial erratic boulder. It was he who first gave the name of 'Cambrian' to one of the earth's strata. He was the son-in-law of James and Frances Williams of Llanfair-yng-Nghornwy.

The magnificent view of Snowdonia from the churchyard, which I admired so much on my first visit, is now obstructed by an immense corrugated asbestos farm shed!

Menai Bridge (PORTHAETHWY).

It is believed Archbishop Baldwin and Gerald the Welshman (Giraldus Cambrensis) landed on Church Island (Llantysilio) when they crossed to Anglesey in 1188 to preach the Crusade, but there is mention of a ferry between Bangor and Porthaethwy as early as 1291. A Ffair y Borth, held annually since the 16th century, is still claimed to be the largest of its kind in Wales. Maps prior to 1811 show the road and ferry used for centuries by the cattle drovers. A house built for the ferryman was later converted into the Cambria Inn, the parlour of which was used for Sunday Schools in the days when it was illegal to conduct them in a private house.

The pleasant little town of Menai Bridge did not grow up until the great Suspension Bridge was built by Telford between 1819 and 1826. It cost £120,000 and measures 579 ft. between the piers and 1,710 ft. overall. The roadway is supported by 16 chains and is raised 100 ft. above the watermark. It is said that when the bridge was finally swung into place Telford synchronized the delicate operation to the music of bagpipes played at either end. It is still the only roadway into Anglesey, although its immense importance as the first bridge from the mainland was overshadowed, 24 years after its completion, by the opening of the Britannia Railway Bridge.

Menai Bridge, backed by low green hills and looking towards the bridge, graceful in spite of its size and strength, and across the Strait to Snowdonia, is reached by a steep road dropping down from the A.5 and too many rush past without realising its interest. The Museum of Childhood, in Water Street, has six rooms of entrancing exhibits covering an enormous range of toys and dolls dating back to the mid-19th century, including a German toy typewriter of 1895, a children's dog-cart of 1850, china, glass-ware and pictures depicting children, or for their use. There is also a Praxinoscope of 1889, magic lanterns, musical boxes and polyphons, most of which can be worked by the insertion of a coin, or are set off at stated intervals.

The Tegfryn Art Gallery, in Cadnant Road, exhibits the works of over 150 North Wales painters. Cadnant Dingle is a wooded valley with an old water-mill.

Church Island is reached by the Belgian Walk, a winding path along the shore of the Strait, constructed by Belgian refugees during the 1914-18 war. The simple little church founded by St. Tysilio in 630 crowns the tiny islet over which its churchyard spreads. In this quiet and lovely retreat lie Sir John Lloyd, the great Welsh historian, and that quaint and lovable character, John Evans (Bardd Cocos, the Cockle Poet) who made his frugal living collecting cockles and is well-remembered by Welsh speakers for his verses, which can best be compared with those of the Scottish poet William McGonagall.

In the Strait, between the Suspension Bridge and the Britannia Bridge, are numerous small islands, with the remains of fish-traps used by the once thriving Menai Fisheries, probably dating from the 16th century. The largest island is Ynys Gorad Goch, which is inhabited. It has an ingenious system of weirs and traps and an old curing tower.

MOELFRE, on the east coast, has grown considerably in recent years, but the old fishing village remains beside the pebble beach. The lifeboat station set up in 1830 has a long list of rescues to its credit. Richard Evans, the coxwain, won his second R.N.L.I. gold medal for gallantry when the crew of eight on board the coaster *Hindlea* was rescued in October 1959, exactly a century after the less fortunate crew and passengers of the *Royal Charter* lost their lives.

Moelfre is the nearest place from which to visit Penrhosllugwy. The church dates in part from 1400. It has an inscribed 6th century stone in the south wall of the chancel and a memorial to Margaret Morris, mother of the Morris brothers of Llanfihangel Tre'r-beirdd.

Within a mile on the north and east of the church are some remarkable remains. The Hen Gapel Llugwy can be seen in a field beside the road to Llugwy Bay. It is approached by stone steps leading down from the roadside. It was built by the Normans during the brief eight years they remained in Anglesey, early in the 12th century. The upper walls were rebuilt in the 14th century and are complete to gable height, although the building is roofless. In the woods just beyond is Din Llugwy, a walled hut group covering half an acre consisting of two circular and seven rectangular buildings, now standing to a maximum height of six ft., which were occupied during the 4th century. The 3,000 years old Llugwy burial chamber, with an 18 ft. capstone - one of the finest in Anglesey - is half a mile away.

NEWBOROUGH is south-east of the Malltraeth Marsh and the great estuary of the Cefni river, where the shining sands left at low tide are broken by shallow pools. They are a haunt of mallards and other wildfowl.

Newborough was given its name by Edward I, when he removed the Welsh population of Llanfaes to make room for the English town and castle of Beaumaris. He granted Newborough a charter and it became a thriving town which sent a member to Parliament in Tudor times, but it is now a quiet village.

Under its original name of Rhosyr it was scarcely less famous than Aberffraw as a resort of the Welsh princes, but even their memory is outshone by its association with Dafydd ap Gwilym, greatest of all the Welsh lyric poets. He flourished in the 14th century and has been called 'the Welsh Dante', with considerable justice. It was at Rhosyr that the auburn haired poet first saw his 'Beatrice' - Morfudd Lawgan. He celebrates in verse his admiration for her; and for the fine church where he attended the Festival of St. Peter.

Rhosyr is now buried beneath the sands of Hendai Forest, but the church remains high on a hill above Newborough. There is the early 14th century chancel and nave Dafydd knew, a 12th century font, and carved sepulchral slabs in the north and south walls, but he would not have seen the tunnel-like effect of the extension in 1600 which makes the aisleless nave and chancel over 90 ft. long, although only just over 16 ft. wide.

There are splendid views of Snowdonia and the Lleyn from the churchyard and from the main street of Newborough. The 19th century half-timbered almshouses and clock tower of the Prichard Jones Institute were given by a local boy who made good in the clothing trade in London.

When I first knew Newborough it was surrounded by one of the largest areas of wind-blown dunes in the west of Britain, with some dunes reaching 60 ft. in height. They were bound together by marram grass (Ammophila arenaria) which for centuries provided material for rope, mat, net and cordage making, which thrived until 1920. The grass was so indispensable, not only for the industry but for the stability of the dunes, that laws were passed to protect it in the reign of Elizabeth I. This industry had already declined when the Forestry Commissioners took over the northern part of Newborough Warren as a National Nature Reserve and planted the dunes with Corsican Pine, and Sitka spruce in the damper areas. Such a transformation of the age-old landscape may seem a desecration to those who remember the fascination of the lonely dunes, and skylarks singing overhead, but it must be remembered the dunes encroached on cornlands even in the time of the Princes of Gwynedd and silted up their landing place at Aber Menai, oldest of the Menai ferries, after a great storm early in the 14th century. The tree-planting here is, in fact, a timely act of preservation.

There are some public rights of way and Nature Trails through the forest and Conservancy area, but written permits must be obtained for other areas. Llanddwyn Island, three miles away, is a low peninsula of Pre-Cambrian rocks which can be reached on foot at all but the highest tides. It has a lighthouse, and a lifeboat station and a row of pilot cottages now used by wardens of the Nature Reserve. They house a Nature Conservancy Council exhibition and a display of local crafts.

The little church of St. Dwynwyn, with its 16th century chancel on the 5th century site of her oratory, is now in ruins but in earlier times both the church and the holy well were famous places of pilgrimage. It was said that the auguries were favourable to lovers if the well bubbled whilst they performed the prescribed ceremonies.

St. Dwynwyn is believed to have been the daughter of the Welsh prince Brychan, from whom the county of Brecon took its name. A plain modern cross near the lighthouse commemorates her, and another modern Celtic cross commemorates those inhabitants of the island who died there.

P ENMON, in the parish of Llangoed, is sheltered by the peninsula jutting out into the sea at the eastern end of the Menai Strait.

Penmon Priory marks the site of a religious settlement believed to have been founded by the brother, or a cousin, of St. Seiriol in the 6th century and given to St. Seiriol when he preached Christianity in the district. The foundations of the Saint's hut are beside the well in which he baptised converts.

The present church bearing his name has a dim, austere Norman nave dating from 1140, lightened by gleaming white-washed walls. The transepts, with a rare sculptured tympanum over the south doorway, a 10th century cross and bold carvings on the tower arches, were rebuilt in 1166-70 after the church had been burnt by Danish raiders. The chancel was added between 1220 and 1240, when Llywelyn the Great gave the Priory to the Prior of Priestholm and the conventual buildings were added when the Priors transferred their seat to Penmon. The ruins of the three-storeyed wing containing the Refectory, with the Dormitory above and a cellar below and a 16th century two-storeyed warming house and kitchen, are substantial, but the Prior's house is much altered and is now a private house.

The huge square dove-cot, with its massive domed roof, had room for nearly a thousand nests. An elaborately carved cross, showing Irish and Scandinavian influences, stands in a field nearby.

The upper part of Llangoed village is particularly attractive, but St. Cawdraf's church has been too drastically restored, including alterations even to the beautifully carved 17th century pulpit. A footpath beside the river drops down-stream to the ruins of Castell Lleiniog, half-hidden in trees near the shingly beach. It was built in 1290 by Hugh of Avranches (The Wolf), Earl of Chester, who with his companion Hugh, Earl of Shrewsbury, committed atrocious crimes against the Welsh before the latter was killed during an attack on the castle by Magnus, King of Norway.

The breezy, lonely headland of Trwyn Du (Black Point) has a lighthouse, built in 1837, which now operates automatically. The old lifeboat station was closed in 1915. The headland is riddled with quarries which provided building material for Beaumaris, the Telford and Stephenson bridges and many other building projects in Anglesey. A mile out to sea is Puffin Island which, as its name implies, is a haunt of puffins and countless other sea birds. It is now uninhabited and can be visited only by written permission. Other names by which the Island has been known tell its history: Priestholm or Ynys Seiriol, from a series of hermits, the first of whom, St. Seiriol, established a monastic settlement there, and Ynys-y-Llygod (Isle of Mice), presumably from the story told by Giraldus Cambrensis that when the island was 'inhabited by hermits, living by manual labour and serving God', if 'by the influence of human passions any discord arises among them all their provisions are devoured and infected by a species of small mice, with which the island abounds; but when the discord ceases, they are no longer molested'. There are the remains of a round tower and of a hermit's oratory on the island.

The puffins declined steadily in numbers, partly because of the mice, but also because they were once considered a delicacy. They were pickled in small barrels and shipped to England and France.

PENMYNYDD, south-east of Llangefni, was the family home of the Tudors, and Plas Penmynydd was probably the birthplace, and certainly the childhood home, of the handsome young squire, Owain Tudor, who captured the heart of a widowed Queen and became the grandfather of Henry VII. The present house dates only from the 16th century.

The church of St. Gredifael, founded in the 6th century, is chiefly of 14th century work but incorporates 12th century masonry from a previous church on the site. The tomb of translucent alabaster bearing the effigies of a mailed knight and his lady, formerly believed to be Ednyfed Fychan, Councillor of Llywelyn the Great and ancestor of Owain Tudor and many other noble North Wales families, is now identified as that of Gronw Tudor, uncle of Owain, Constable of Beaumaris Castle in 1382 and close friend of the Black Prince. The tomb has suffered from a belief that chips from it gave relief in eye treatment.

Almshouses originally built in 1620 have been modernised internally to provide five modern dwellings.

Several English monarchs showed a keen interest in Penmynydd. Elizabeth I purchased her annual supply of honey there and Queen Victoria contributed to the restoration of the church.

RED WHARF BAY (TRAETH COCH), a sandy bay on the east coast, is five miles across at low tide. It is protected on the west by Dwlban Point, on the cliffs of which is Castell Mawr, the site of a British encampment where Roman coins have been found. The Bay remains unspoilt, with its caravan site discreetly hidden. On the east is the headland crowned by Din Sylwy.

Llanddona church, on the east of the bay, was rebuilt in 1873 at a total cost of 'barely £600' by the Rev. Peter Jones who 'acted as secretary and treasurer . . . furnished the plans and acted as Clerk of the Works'.

The Bay is a traditional landing place of witches cast adrift from Ireland. A large quarry was worked there in the 19th century and a small ship-yard built ships for the Amlwch copper trade. Railway enthusiasts are intrigued by the railway line from Red Wharf Bay, which is referred to in all standard works on early railways but which Kenneth Brown has proved was a 'Ghost' railway, existing only on paper in spite of the Act of Parliament authorising its construction.

Pentraeth is shown on early 17th century maps at the head of the bay, but is now on reclaimed land a mile inland at a cross-road. It has seen considerable building activity in recent years but is still a pleasant village on a small stream and surrounded by low, grassy gorse-covered hills. East of the village, woodlands rise from the bay to 500 ft. Lon-y-Bwbach (Hobgoblin's Lane) is said to be haunted by the ghost of a Royalist soldier killed in the Civil War.

There are a number of large houses in the

neighbourhood. The red brick Georgian mansion, incongruously named Plas Gwyn (White House), became the seat of the Panton family in the 18th century when Paul Panton, a lawyer and antiquary, married the heiress, Margaret Griffiths. He was a patron of the bard, Evan Evans (Ieuan Fardd), and is mentioned in the letters of the Morris brothers. Marian and Bodeilio date from about 1600 and Plas Llanddyfnan from the 16th century, with 18th and 19th century alterations.

RHOSCOLYN, on the south-west coast of Holy Island, has two very secluded sandy bays, some sea-weed covered rocks and fine cliff scenery. The village lies a mile inland, with a steep winding lane down to the shore. China Clay was quarried there in the 19th century and Rhoscolyn marble was used in building Worcester, Bristol and Peterborough cathedrals. There was also a large oyster industry there at the end of the Victorian era.

The doorway of the church was reset in the south wall when the church was rebuilt in 1875 and the 15th century font was preserved. St. Gwynfaen, who founded the church in the 6th century, had a holy well on a headland west of the church which is still in an unusually good state of preservation. A low stone on the cliffs near Rhoscolyn commemorates Tyger, a retriever dog which saved four lives at the cost of his own, when a ketch sank in a fog off Maen Piscar rock. He swam the three-quarters of a mile to the coast four times, guiding each of the men to safety, but died from exhaustion when the last man was saved.

RHOSNEIGR, on the west coast of Anglesey, between the sea and Llyn Maelog, is reached by the A.4080, which completely encircles the lake. Rhosneigr, which has grown considerably in recent years, has a wide sandy bay in which are several small islands, north of which is Traeth Crigyll where a famous - or rather, infamous - band of wreckers lured many ships to destruction. They were tried for their crimes in Beaumaris in 1741 and are commemorated in a popular Welsh ballad, *Crogi Lladron Crigyll* (the hanging of the thieves of Crigyll), by Lewis Morris. The rebuilt parish church, founded in 605, is in the village of Llanfaelog, east of the reedy, bird-haunted Llyn Maelor. A mural preserved from an earlier church on the site commemorates 'The fifty-six unfortunate persons who lost their lives in crossing the River Menai on the Fatal 5th day of December, 1785'. North-east from Llanfaelog is Tŷ Newydd burial chamber which was excavated in 1935, yielding fragments of pottery and a flint arrow-head which may indicate the use of the chamber in the early Bronze Age.

Rhosneigr had a thriving ship-building industry as early as 1787 on the shores of the lake.

The name of Rhosneigr may be derived from 'Rhos' (a moor) and the name of some now unknown person, although it has also been said it is from Rhos-y-Neidr (moor of the adder). More certain is the fascination of the Tywyn Trewin, north of Rhosneigr, which reaches away to the Valley airfield, covering 7,400 acres of gorse and sand-dunes with interesting flora and bird-life.

TREARDDUR. Until the beginning of this century, almost the only house in Trearddur was Towyn Lodge, a Georgian house in which Telford lived when building the Anglesey section of the London road, but the attractions of the wide sandy bay, with its rocky outcrops and low cliffs, drew increasing numbers of summer visitors. It still offers outdoor sports rather than more sophisticated amusements. Between Trearddur and Roscolyn, three miles or so farther south along the west coast of Holy Isle, there are two fine natural rock arches.

Trearddur is the nearest point to the tumbled stones of Trefignath burial chamber, of the 'segmented cist' type, with a continuous passage 45 ft. long, more easily discerned by the expert than by most visitors. The chapel of St. Ffraid (St. Bridget) once stood on a mound in the centre of the bay, and there are the remains of a 6th century chapel half a mile to the east.

VALLEY. The famous R.A.F. Station was established at Valley in 1941, and was used as a Night Fighter and Air-Sea Rescue base and also as a reception airfield for American bomber aircraft flown over from the United States of America. It is now a permanent R.A.F. Station and an emergency airport for civilian aircraft, with innumerable rescues to the credit of its daring pilots. It has the only advanced jet flying school in the R.A.F., and a Strike Command Missile Practice Camp. The name Valley is thought to have been given by Telford when constructing his Holyhead road. It is a literal description of the area.

It was when bulldozers were levelling the site for the airfield that the great Llyn Cerrig Bach hoard was discovered. The bronze and iron objects date from the 2nd century B.C. to the 1st century A.D. and include chariot-fittings, horse harness, weapons, tools and iron gang-chains for slaves or prisoners of war, all showing astonishing technical perfection. The embossed plaque and engraved shield-boss are among the finest examples of the La Tène style yet found in Britain. The hoard is believed to have been a relic of the last stand of the Druids in Anglesey, chronicled by Tacitus. It is now in the National Museum of Wales at Cardiff, where there is also a scale model of a British war chariot of the 1st century B.C., based on evidence found at Llyn Cerrig Bach and other chariot burials.

SIR GAERNARFON (CAERNARFONSHIRE)

ABER, on the coast east of Bangor, is a pleasant place made enchanting by its background of wooded hills rising to the towering outline of the Carnedd range and by the view northwards across the Menai Strait to the Anglesey coast and Ynys Seiriol (Puffin Island). Aber's full name, hardly ever used now, is the more poetical Abergwyngregyn (Mouth of the River of White Shells).

The farm acquired by the University College of North Wales in 1916 is at Aber. It is now a highly successful centre for agricultural experiments and teaching.

A mound in the village is believed to be the site of a castle first built by the Normans and later by Llywelyn ab Iowerth (the Great). There is a delightful walk up a two mile long wooded valley to the Aber falls. The two falls tumbling over high precipices a quarter of a mile apart can be reached only by walking. The rocks on either side are too dangerous for any but the most expert climbers, but there are numerous good mountain walks in the area.

Aber has one of the many legends of a drowned village common along the Welsh coast, but the supposed site exposed at low tide has a natural origin. It is due to glacial action during the great Ice Age.

ABERDARON, the most distant village on the Lleyn (Llŷn), is a place of closely clustering houses and cottages with narrow streets and a church so close to the shore that the sea laps the churchyard wall at high tide, and the pale gold sand of the magnificent, windy beach is blown into the churchyard. The church was founded in the 6th century by St. Hywyn, Confessor to St. Cadfan, first Abbot of Bardsey, but dates from the 12th century. It was enlarged three centuries later and has a weather-worn Norman doorway.

Aberdaron is the natural port for Bardsey Island (Ynys Enlli) and it was here the pilgrims flocked to wait for a favourable crossing to 'The Isle of Saints'. The Old Kitchen, or Gegin Fawr (Great Kitchen), was built in the 14th century as a rest house for the pilgrims and is now a café and souvenir shop for tourists. The Post Office was designed by Sir Clough Williams-Ellis. There is an attractive stone bridge with arched parapets across the little Afon Daron.

The most memorable native of Aberdaron, Richard Jones (Dic of Aberdaron), was born there in 1788. He had no schooling but managed to teach himself 13 languages and 25 dialects. He compiled a dictionary of Welsh, Greek and Hebrew, the manuscript of which is now in St. Asaph cathedral. Always eccentric and never practical, he was unable to use his gifts to better his financial position and died at St. Asaph in 1843 in penury.

The headland beyond Aberdaron Bay is the most westerly point of Caernarfonshire, with a magnificent coast line, much of which is in the care of the National Trust. Ffynnon Fair, on the seashore below Mynydd Mawr, is covered at high tide but when uncovered at ebb tide its waters remain clear and pure. On the cliffs above is the site of Capel Mair, an ancient chapel said to have been built for the use of mariners. A folk tale tells of a beautiful lady who was visited by a 'strange lady' who told her that her greatest wish would be gratified if she ascended the dangerous cliff path with a pitcher of water from the well and walked once round the church without losing a single drop of water - but does not relate whether she was successful.

The white sands of Porthorion beach, 2½ miles from Aberdaron, make a strange whistling noise if walked upon after they have been dried by the sun. North of Porthorion is Carreg Hall, a former home of Welsh Chieftains, and Mynydd Carreg. The disused Carreg quarries of jasper and pink marble supplied building material for numerous public buildings in London and other cities. Some of the roads in the neighbourhood of Carreg are paved with coloured marble from the quarries.

East of Aberdaron are: Bodwrdda, an Elizabethan mansion acquired by the Edwards family in 1749, and just visible from the road; Porth Ysgo, where the National Trust has a beautiful area of cliffs, waterfall and streams, looking towards Ynys Gwylan Fawr and Ynys Gwylan Fach (Seagull Islands); and the Plas-yn-Rhiw estate on the west shore of the wide Porth Neigwl (Hell's Mouth). It was given to the National Trust by the Keating sisters in memory of their parents. The manor-house, partly Tudor and partly earlier, with Georgian additions, was uninhabited for 15 years but has been restored, together with its gardens and Sarn Rhiw, a traditional Welsh cottage. Most of this area has been scheduled by the Nature Conservancy, and no shooting for sport or picking of wild flowers is permitted.

North-east of Aberdaron, on or near the B.4413 to Llanbedrog, are Bryncroes, which has an ancient church with some curious wooden memorials to the Trygan family, Mellteyrn Sarn, Mellteyrn and Botwnnog.

Mellteyrn was the birthplace of Henry Rowlands in 1551. He bequeathed funds for the establishment of a grammar school at Botwnnog.

Sarn Mellteyrn is in a sheltered valley half-way between Aberdaron and Abersoch. Roy Campbell, South Africa's greatest poet, lived at Tŷ Corn, an old cottage in Sarn Mellteyrn, in 1922 with his wife Mary soon after their marriage, while he finished his first book, *The Flaming Terrapin*. Their daughter, Tess, was born there.

ABERSOCH, on the south coast of Lleyn, at the mouth of a trout stream, has sands, rocks, a good harbour, a glen with all the luxuriant vegetation of a Devon combe, and views of St. Tudwal's Islands and mountain-ringed Cardigan Bay.

St. Tudwal's Islands were bought in 1956 by Sir Clough Williams-Ellis, to save them from exploitation. Both are now bird sanctuaries, and visitors cannot land without special permission. There is an abandoned lighthouse on St. Tudwal's Island East and the remains of a 12th century chapel which may mark the site of a 6th century oratory founded by the Breton St. Tudwal, bishop of Treguir, on St. Tudwal's Island West.

South-west of Abersoch is Llanengan. The Perpendicular church with its square tower is one of the finest and most interesting in Lleyn. It has a double nave, two splendidly carved rood-screens and rood-lofts, and a solid oak coffer in which St. Peter's Pence were stored.

It is said that more than half the houses in Llanengan and the Abersoch yachting centre are second homes, with a sadly disruptive effect on the local way of life.

Llangian, north-west of Abersoch, is an attractive village beside a stream. It has a long, narrow church restored in the Victorian era. In the churchyard is a 6th century pillar stone with a Latin inscription to Melus the Doctor - believed to be the only record of a *medicus* on an early Christian monument in Britain.

The diminutive and very secluded Capel Newydd, dating from 1769, is the earliest surviving Nonconformist chapel in North Wales. Nearby is the entrance to the Nanhoron Valley with its woods and meadows.

Also north of Abersoch is Castellmarch, a 17th century manor-house with an unusual porch and thick oak rafters, which is now a farm-house. It is said to mark the site of the castle of King March, who had horses' ears. He put to death every barber who attended him, in order to keep his secret, but it was eventually revealed when a piper made pipes from the reeds growing above their graves. The pipes sang of the king's secret when the piper played. The legend is said to originate from the fact that 'march' is Welsh for 'horse', but the story is common to many countries.

BANGOR. The crowded streets of the cathedral city of Bangor reflect its importance as an ecclesiastical, cultural, tourist and commercial centre.

Both the town and the cathedral have had a chequered history of burning and rebuilding, and only a few ancient buildings remain in the narrow valley which is hemmed in by steep hills and dominated by the impressive modern University College of North Wales on the wooded height of Penallt ridge. The modern town reaches to the shore of the Menai Strait on the north-west and to the sea on the north coast at Garth.

Bangor cathedral is on one of the oldest ecclesiastical sites in Britain. It was founded in 546 by St. Deiniol, 52 years before Canterbury was founded by St. Augustine. There was a monastery on the site as early as 525 and it is believed there were Celtic bishops in North Wales even before the time of St. Deiniol.

In spite of the many re-buildings down the centuries, there are still traces of the Norman cathedral built in 1120-1139. The aisle walls and north and south doorways are mid-14th century and the nave, clerestory and western tower are early 16th century. It was thoroughly restored by Sir Gilbert Scott and his son.

Three 12th century Welsh princes and 11 bishops were buried in the cathedral, and there are memorials to a number of famous Welshmen. A 14th century sepulchral slab with the effigy of a lady is known as the 'Eva' slab, from its inscription.

The Mostyn Christ, carved in oak, is on permanent loan from Lord Mostyn. It dates from 1518 and is of a rare type, representing Christ seated on a rock, bound and wearing a crown of thorns.

The earliest mention of an organ in the cathedral is

found in the Commendatory Ode addressed by Dafydd ap Gwilym to Hywel, Dean of Bangor, about 1360. It has been replaced several times since then.

Among the manuscripts owned by the cathedral are a copy of Bishop Hoadley's sermon, which caused the Bangor Controversy in 1717, and the beautifully illustrated manuscript, Bishop Anian's Pontifical, containing services which only a bishop could administer. It is not certain whether it was compiled for Bishop Anian I, who held the See from 1267 to 1305, or for Bishop Anian II, who was bishop of Bangor from 1309 to 1327/8, but there is a tradition that it was used when Anian I christened the first English Prince of Wales in 1284.

The Bishop's palace, on the north-west of the cathedral, dates from the 16th to 17th centuries with some later additions. The last Bishop to live there was Daniel Lewis Lloyd, Bishop of Bangor from 1890 to 1899. It is now the Town Hall.

The Gardd yr Esgob (Bishop's Garden) has been laid out as a 'Bible Garden'. It is a typically Welsh conception, for Welsh men and women still draw much of their inspiration from the Bible. On the south side of the 'Bible Walk' are plants traditionally associated with Christian festivals, saints and prophets. On the north side they are arranged chronologically from Genesis to Revelation. The Creation is represented by primitive grasses and cereals, recorded from the upper reaches of the Euphrates 5,000 years ago, and wheat from Egypt. These are followed by every tree, shrub and plant mentioned in the Bible which can be induced to grow in the open in Bangor, including those shrubs and trees in King Solomon's garden - and it is astonishing how many rare plants flourish here.

Enjoyment of the garden is greatly enhanced by reference to Tatham Whitehead's Official Handbook, which is well illustrated, fully annotated, and keyed to a very clear map.

Caernarfon Castle

Photo: British Tourist Authority

Plas Mawr, Conwy, Caernarfonshire

Photo: Wales Tourist Board

The Bible Garden has created world-wide interest and has been copied near Sydney, Australia, and the Brooklyn Botanical Gardens, U.S.A. have asked the Bangor Council for assistance in creating a similar Bible Garden in the region of New York.

It was Bangor's importance as a commercial centre after the formation of Penrhyn Port at the mouth of the Afon Cegin, following the development of the Penrhyn quarries in 1782, which resulted, at long last, in the granting of a Charter to Bangor a century later.

The University College was established in Bangor in 1884. It was the third of the constituent colleges of the University of Wales. The Bangor School of scholars and poets, inspired by (Sir) John Morris-Jones, who was appointed the first lecturer of Welsh there in 1889 and had a Chair of Welsh created for him in 1894, began a Welsh literary revival, the effect of which has lasted to the present day. (Sir) John E. Lloyd, who became Professor of History in 1899, had an equally great influence on Welsh historial studies.

BARDSEY ISLAND (YNYS ENLLI), a mile or two across Bardsey Sound from Aberdaron, had a great reputation as a place of pilgrimage, particularly after the monks of Bangor Is-coed fled there after their monastery was sacked following the Battle of Chester in 615, but seems to have been the site of a religious community founded by St. Cadfan at least a hundred years earlier. Known as the 'Isle of Saints' in the days when any especially holy man, particularly a monk, was given the name of 'Saint', it was reputedly the burial place of 20,000 saints and was so venerated - and so difficult of approach across the dangerous currents of Bardsey Sound - that three pilgrimages there counted as a pilgrimage to Rome.

Among its many legends is an old belief that Merlin lies sleeping there in a glass house, with the Thirteen Treasures of Britain, until the reappearance of King Arthur in time of need.

The island is a mile long and half-a-mile wide, and the whole area amounts only to 444 acres, half of which is low-lying farmland and the other half a hill rising to 548 ft. The short springy turf is ideal for sheep grazing. In 1870-5 the third Baron Newborough, who owned Bardsey, re-housed the then thriving farming-fishing community in model farms. Owing to the difficulty of communicating with the mainland he also appointed a headman to administer the affairs of the island who became known as the 'King of Bardsey'. The 'dynasty' continued until just before the 1939-45 war.

There are the ruins of a 13th century monastery on Bardsey and a lighthouse designed by John Nelson in 1821. A Celtic cross of Anglesey marble marks the grave of Lord Newborough, who died in 1888, and a small cross commemorates the 20,000 saints.

Bardsey is now a sanctuary for countless migrating birds and for the great colonies of sea birds nesting there. The old schoolhouse is used by the Bardsey Bird and Field Observatory and the island is now an important ringing station.

BEDDGELERT, 12½ miles south-east of Caernarfon, at the junction of the A.4055 and the A.498, is a typical Welsh mountain village of stone-built, slate-roofed houses in a wonderful setting of woods, meadows, rushing streams and towering mountains in the heart of Snowdonia National Park. It stands at the confluence of the Afon Colwyn, Afon Gwynant, and the upper reaches of the Afon Glaslyn, with Llyn Gwynant, Llyn Dinas and the lovely Aberglaslyn Pass nearby.

Many coach parties visit the 'grave of Gelert', from which Beddgelert is said to derive its name, but, as Israel Zangwill says:

'Pass on, O tender-hearted, dry your eyes;
Not here a greyhound, but a landlord lies'.

The story originated in 1801, when David Prichard, the publicity-minded landlord of the Royal Goat Inn, with the help of two friends, set up a cairn in a meadow 1¼ miles from Beddgelert to support the 'legend' in which Llywelyn, on seeing the blood of a wolf which Gelert had killed, flew into a rage and killed the dog, believing it had killed his baby son. Prichard gave the details to the Hon. William Spencer, who composed the well-known ballad, *Gellert*, which resulted in a profitable increase in the number of visitors to Beddgelert. The name of the village is in all probability derived from a Celtic priory commemorating St. Celert, which grew up to cater for pilgrims to Bardsey Island. The 13th century church, largely restored in the Victorian era, was the chapel of an Augustinian priory.

William Jones (Bleddyn) was born in Beddgelert in 1829. His father was John Jones, the sexton, who is referred to in Charles Kingsley's *Two Years Ago*. Bleddyn spent his working hours behind a draper's counter but all his leisure as an antiquary, local historian, geologist and collector of folk-lore. He provided the Rev. David Erwyd Jenkins with much of the material for *Bedd Gelert, Facts and Fancies*, published in 1899. Beddgelert was also the birthplace of David Ffrancon Davies, the distinguished singer, who was the father of Miss Gwen Ffrancon-Davies. Dafydd Nantmor, or Nanmor, a 15th century bard, was born in the neighbouring village of Nantmor.

Visitors to the Goat Inn have ranged from Coleridge to Prince Arthur of Connaught, and A.J. Froude entertained Matthew Arnold and Charles Kingsley at Nant Gwynant.

A mile north of the village is the Beddgelert National Forest Park. Dinas Emrys, south of Llyn Dinas, is an Iron Age hill fort later used by the Romans, where bronze harness ringed with iron bars, and other relics have been found. It has long been associated with legends of a dragon which prevented the building of Vortigern's palace. His magicians told him to sacrifice a fatherless boy, but the intended victim had the gift of prophecy and revealed a pool beneath the site where the conquest of a white dragon by a red dragon symbolised a final victory. When asked his name, the boy said 'I am called Ambrosius'. The story is told by Nennius and has been confused with Gildas's account of Ambrosius, a 5th century hero who is said to have defeated the Saxons and, according to Welsh tradition, was known as Emrys Wledig (Ruler), from whom Dinas Emrys took its name. Geoffrey of Monmouth further confuses the issue by identifying Ambrosius with Merlin 'who was also called Ambrosius'.

Beddgelert is the nearest starting point for Moel Hebog (Hawk Hill), 2,566 ft. high, which gives a magnificent view of the Snowdon massif.

BETHESDA is 4 miles south-east of Bangor on the A.5, at the confluence of the Afon Ogwen and Afon Llafar, with a background of some of the grandest scenery of Snowdonia at the northern end of the Nant Ffrancon Pass.

It is a quarrying village of slate debris, dominated on the south by the vast Penrhyn Quarries which are not the least striking feature of the landscape. Terraces 60 ft. high have been hewn out of the northern end of Bron Lwyd in the Glyder range, forming an amphitheatre 1,140 ft. deep. It is believed to be the largest slate quarry in the world.

Slate was quarried at Penrhyn at least as early as the reign of Elizabeth I but it remained a village industry until the 18th century, when the heiress of Penrhyn married Richard Pennant, who had valuable estates in Jamaica and was a distant kinsman of Thomas Pennant, the naturalist and traveller. Richard Pennant spent hundreds of thousands of pounds installing machinery and constructing a tramway to Port Penrhyn. At the height of their productivity the quarries employed hundreds of men, and with the enormous fortune he gained by his systematic development he built Penrhyn Castle for himself and model homes for the workers on the estate. He was created Baron Penrhyn in 1783.

The splitting and cutting of slates calls for extremely skilled craftsmanship. The various sizes are known by the trade names of 'queens', 'duchesses', 'countesses' and 'ladies', and the colours range through shades of blue, green and red. They are still in demand, although on a much smaller scale. Groups of visitors are shown round by a guide, by previous arrangement, from April to September.

Lord Penrhyn also set an example of agricultural development in an area which was then one of the most backward of Welsh counties. He built roads, planted waste lands with trees, and provided better farm-houses for his tenants.

The original name of Bethesda was Glan Ogwen, after the river which runs through it, but when the Nonconformists built Bethesda Chapel it completely superseded the older name. It is a great centre of Nonconformity, with many handsome chapels and a tradition of choral singing and a respect for education which has produced a fine breed of Welshmen.

BETWS-Y-COED is on the A.5, at the meeting of the Conwy, Lledr and Llugwy valleys, famous for their waterfalls. Surrounded by the great Gwydir Forest, it is one of the best known of all the beauty spots of Snowdonia. Its scenery has been painted and photographed countless times and paintings of it have been hung at many Royal Academy Exhibitions since it was 'discovered' in the 18th century. The signboard painted by David Cox, who visited Betws annually from 1844 to 1856, is preserved in the Royal Oak Hotel.

Pont-y-Pair (Bridge of the Cauldron), which spans the Afon Llugwy on the Capel Curig side of the village, is said to have been designed by a Welsh mason, Howel, who died about 1740 before the work was finished. Farther up the same river is the wooden ladder-like Miners' Bridge, originally built to enable miners to cross from Pentre Du to mines on the hills opposite, where at one time 500 hands were employed. It is another mile to the famous Swallow Falls.

The Old Church, which is very small and quite unspoilt, has a medieval font and a very fine 14th century effigy of a Welsh knight in studded armour of a kind rarely to be seen. The Latin inscription identifies him as Gruffydd, son of Dafydd Goch. He was the great-nephew of Llywelyn, the last Welsh Prince of Wales. The church is used now only for weddings and funerals.

The handsome cast-iron Waterloo Bridge was built by Telford in the year the battle of Waterloo was fought.

The Conwy Valley Railway Museum has exhibits reflecting many aspects of railway life and work, with special emphasis on the railways of North Wales. The small exhibits are in a specially designed building in the Old Goods Yard of the British Rail station, and the standard gauge railway stock is displayed nearby.

BODNANT GARDEN, four miles south of Conwy, was in Denbighshire until the alteration in administrative boundaries in 1974. The world-famous garden, incorporating large native trees, was laid out in 1875 by Henry Pochin. It has been splendidly maintained and imaginatively enlarged by his descendants and was given to the National Trust in 1949 by his great-grandson, the second Lord Aberconway. It covers 87 acres and is especially celebrated not only for its rhododendrons and camellias but also for its series of terraces above the Afon Conwy, each commanding magnificent views of Snowdonia.

The aim has always been to have a wide range of interesting and beautiful plants suited to the climate and the soil rather than to make a botanical collection. Pochin planted most of the conifers, a number of shrubs and formal beds and the remarkable Laburnum Arch,

which is an almost unbelievably lovely 'tunnel' of golden
tassels swaying in the slightest breeze when it is in bloom.

The Pin Mill incorporated in the garden was originally
constructed about 1730 at Woodchester in
Gloucestershire as a Garden House and later used as a
mill for the manufacture of pins. It was rescued from
decay in 1938 and removed to Bodnant.

CAERNARFON (Y GAER YN ARFON), The Fort on
the Shore, is at the mouth of the Afon Seiont, on the
south-west of the Menai Strait.

The Roman fort of Segontium was at Llanbeblig, half
a mile south-east of present day Caernarfon which was
founded by Edward I in 1284. Laws were enacted to
exclude any Welsh people from living there but it now
proudly claims to be intensely Welsh, which no one is
likely to dispute who has listened to the many Welsh
speakers, especially in Y Maes, the central square, on
market day.

The magnificent castle dominating Y Maes covers
three acres and has walls between seven and nine feet
thick. It is so impressive from any viewpoint that most
sightseers agree with Dr. Johnson, who was startled into
abandoning his usual disparaging remarks on buildings
in Wales and wrote in his *Journal* 'The castle is an edifice
of stupendous magnitude and strength. To survey it
would take much time. I did not think there had been
such buildings; it surpassed my ideas'. An American
visitor, A. Cleveland Cook, who arrived on an excursion
steamer from Menai Bridge in 1851, says in his
Impressions of England: '. . . when, at last, the old walls of
Caernarvon rose before my sight in all their feudal
grandeur and historic dignity I felt like one inspired with
rapture, though not the less impressed with a sense of
something awful and august . . . its towers are really
stupendous . . .'.

The accounts show that Caernarfon cost £19,000 to
build - the equivalent of about two million pounds of

present day money - and that an extraordinarily cosmopolitan crowd of architects, military engineers, craftsmen and labourers were employed. They were recruited from every English county and from all over Europe.

Under later kings the castle's importance declined and by the time Richard II stayed there, during his wanderings after Bolingbroke landed in England in 1399, it was unfurnished and he had only straw to lie on. It was garrisoned during the rising of Owain Glyndŵr and his men were twice repulsed. It changed hands three times during the Civil War but was held by the parliamentarians against the final attack by the royalist Sir John Owen of Clenennau. After the Restoration it was allowed to crumble into ruin until, in the 19th century, the work of restoration was begun. It was scheduled as an Ancient Monument and to-day it is outwardly as strong and impressive as ever. Only from the inside can it be seen that it is partly roofless, although it is still possible to walk around the battlements. There is an interesting Regimental Museum in the Queen's Tower which illustrates the history of the Royal Welch Fusiliers from the foundation of the regiment in 1689 to the present day. Exhibits include the 16lb. Russian Bell Gun captured at the Battle of the Alma in 1854, the keys of Corunna, handed over after the town's surrender in the Peninsular War, an example of the Mitre hats worn by the soldiers in 1750, and a collection of medals.

The legend that the first English Prince of Wales, afterwards Edward II, was born in the Eagle tower of the castle has been disproved, but he was born in the town and traditionally presented to the Welsh people in the castle. In 1900, over 600 years later, Edward of Windsor (afterwards Duke of Windsor), was invested in the castle - the first English Prince of Wales to be invested in Wales. H.R.H. Prince Charles was invested there by H.M. the Queen in a colourful ceremony which I had the privilege of witnessing in 1967.

Almost all the 13th century town walls of Caernarfon remain. St. Mary's church, on the curtain wall in the north-west angle, was probably the garrison church. There has inevitably been much rebuilding inside the walls but the modern street plan coincides exactly with Speed's map of 1610. There are numerous good Georgian houses and several ancient inns. Y Maes, with its constant coming and going of buses labelled to all parts of North Wales, has been made even busier since the railway station was closed.

Y Maes, beneath the castle walls, is presided over by Sir William Goscombe John's statue of Lloyd George (afterwards first Earl of Dwyfor) in a characteristic declamatory pose. It was unveiled in 1921 by W.M. Hughes, then Prime Minister of Australia.

Even before the days of the Romans there was a settlement on Twthill Rock although little remains beyond three Neolithic axes and Bronze Age relics, now in the National Museum of Wales.

The first Roman fort of Segontium dates from about A.D.78. It has been partially excavated and the foundations left exposed, enabling the ground plan to be seen clearly. There is a small Museum of relics found on the site including an inscribed altar to Minerva. The lower Roman fort was built about A.D.350, closer to the estuary.

In its day the Roman fortress excited as much awe and amazement as Caernarfon castle, and the memory lingered and was magnified in the Welsh folk tale, *The Dream of Macsen Wledig*, included in *The Mabinogion*.

Llanbeblig church, dedicated to St. Peblig, 'the son of Helen and Magnus Maximus', dates from the 14th century. The Vaynol chapel contains the finest altar tomb in Caernarfonshire and some good heraldic brasses.

CAPEL CURIG, 600 ft. above sea level, on the A.5, is hemmed in by mountains. It is one of the oldest resorts of Snowdonia but is still a small, straggling village where the

Afon Gwryd meets the Afon Llugwy.

Capel Curig is one of the best centres for climbing Moel Siabod, Tryfan and the foothills of the Glyders, and there is trout fishing in the Afon Llugwy and in the Llynnau Mymbr - two lakes linked by a short channel.

Four miles farther along the Bangor Road and nearer Snowdon, at the head of the wild Llanberis Pass, is Penygwryd, the famous climbers' inn described in Kingsley's *Two Years Ago*. It is now a National Mountaineering Centre of the Central Council for Physical Recreation and offers courses on mountain craft, hill walking, rock climbing, canoeing and other outdoor activities.

J.M.A. Thomson, a schoolmaster from Llandudno, who began climbing in the 1890's, was the leading Welsh climber until his death in 1921, but many other famous climbers have tackled the steep rock faces which provide such testing work that they have long been a training ground for climbs in the Alps and the Himalayas. It was here Sir Edmund Hillary and others trained for their successful ascent of Everest. It cannot be emphasised too strongly that these climbs are not for beginners, especially not for those with inadequate equipment.

Visits to the National Nature Reserves at Cwm Idwal and Cwm Glan, Crafnant, with their rich flora, can be made only by those undertaking serious studies and even then only after a permit has been issued by the Nature Conservancy headquarters for Wales at Bangor.

CLYNNOG FAWR is a pretty coastal village of the Lleyn, on the A.499 from Caernarfon to Pwllheli, with an outstandingly fine and spacious late Perpendicular church. Leland visited it in 1536 and thought it 'the fayrest church yn al Cairnarvonshire'.

The church is dedicated to St. Beuno, who founded several monasteries in Wales but made his principal establishment here. There are more churches and chapels dedicated to St. Beuno in North Wales than to any other saint. He died at Clynnog Fawr c.630, where he is believed to have been buried, and is best remembered for the tradition that he restored to life his niece Gwenfrewi (St. Winifred) of Holywell, Flintshire.

The monastery became a collegiate building in 1291 but lost its collegiate status at the Dissolution. It has a spacious North porch, a panelled roof with intricately carved flowers at the joints, a beautifully restored screen and 14 original prebendary stalls with book-desks. The little St. Beuno's Chapel is reached through a passage from under the tower. It was used as a schoolroom between 1827 and 1849 by Ebenezer Thomas (Eben Fardd), a poet and schoolmaster born at Llanarmon, another Lleyn village, south of Clynnog. St. Beuno's shrine was destroyed by fire in 1856. The chapel was restored in 1913 when the foundations of an older building were discovered.

St. Beuno's Chest is an ancient dug-out chest used to store the offerings of pilgrims on their way to Bardsey Island and the fees paid by the owners of new born calves and lambs with the so-called 'Nod Beuno' (St. Beuno's ear-mark). The tall narrow slab with a sundial incised with time measurements of the style used in Ireland and Anglo-Saxon England, and dating from the 11th or early 12th century, is the only example of the type known in Wales.

St. Beuno's well, west of the church, is a substantial structure with stone benches, steps down to the water and niches in the east wall, and is surrounded by walls 6 ft. high.

There is an impressive Neolithic burial chamber between the well and the cliff-edge.

Conwy, on the north coast, at the mouth of the Afon Conwy, is the most perfect of the walled towns surviving in Britain, with a castle which is a triumph of military architecture unsurpassed in Europe. Although this necessarily means that its streets are very congested in the height of the season until the long awaited by-pass materializes, this is compensated for by the sense of long continuity. This is no reconstruction but a living community with its roots in the past. The walls are about 1¾ miles in length and, either by accident or design, are in the shape of a Welsh harp, with the castle at the base. There are 21 towers, three double-towered gateways and a spur projecting 60 yards from the quay. Conwy was once famous for its pearl fisheries, which are mentioned by Tacitus and in Spenser's *Faerie Queene*.

Outstanding among the surviving ancient houses is Aberconwy, which now belongs to the National Trust. It has massive stone walls, and the great oak ceiling joists of the ground floor are believed to date from the 14th century. There is an outside staircase to the upper storey. Across the road is the Black Lion, a former coaching inn, which bears the date 1569, and the rebuilt Blue Bell, on the site of the building where the annual meetings of the Court Leet of the manor of Nant Conwy were held. Another house in Castle Street, once the home of the Hookes family, still has a carved beam under an upper window.

The huge Elizabethan Town House, Plas Mawr, has such a rabbit-warren of passages that it is easy to get lost in it. It was built in 1577 by Robert Wynn, and the splendid plasterwork resembles that in Gwydir House, near Llanrwst. Robert Wynn was the uncle of the first Sir John Wynn of Gwydir, and his adventurous career is detailed in Sir John's *History of the Gwydir Family*. The 'Ghost room', about which many strange stories have been told, has a projecting lantern window overlooking the courtyard with its well. There is much fine period furniture in the large rooms. Plas Mawr has been the headquarters of the Royal Cambrian Academy of Art since 1877.

The queer little house on the Quay, which is the unchallenged 'smallest house in Britain', measures only 6 ft. in width, 8 ft. 4 ins. in length and 9 ft. 4 ins. in height. It has two storeys and is crammed with mid-Victorian

Welsh furniture, ornaments and brasses. The last tenant, who lived for many years in this small house, was over 6 ft. in height!

The parish church was originally part of the Cistercian Abbey at Aberconwy, founded by Llywelyn the Great in 1172. Several of the Welsh princes were buried there, including Llywelyn himself, but their graves are now unidentifiable. The abbey was plundered and partly destroyed by English soldiers under Henry III and was removed to Maenan, eight miles away up the Conwy Valley, by Edward I when he began building the town and castle. Parts of the 12th century abbey church were incorporated in the 14th century reconstruction, and some of the stonework of the abbey is believed to survive in the walling of the hotel yard of the Castle Hotel in High Street.

St. Mary's has a magnificent 15th century carved wooden screen, a Tudor font, in which Archbishop John Williams was christened, and a cross of early Byzantine workmanship, believed to have been used in Monza cathedral, Italy, from the 7th to the 18th centuries. There is much fine stone and wood carving and the monuments include an effigy, said to be Mary Williams, mother of the Archbishop or his daughter, and a 17th century floor slab to Nicholas Hookes which tells us he was the 41st son of his father and himself the father of 27 children. A marble bust commemorates John Gibson, the great Victorian sculptor.

The grave in the churchyard associated with Wordsworth's poem *We are Seven* is easily recognizable by its covering of an iron grille topped by seven fleur-de-lys. By a strange coincidence two other graves, a few yards away, each record the deaths of the seven children of each of two local families.

At the top of Chapel Street are the foundations of the Parlwr Mawr, the palace of Archbishop John Williams, the most famous native of Conwy. It was demolished in 1948. This remarkable but controversial man was appointed Lord Keeper of the Seal by James I, but after the king's death he incurred the enmity of the Duke of Buckingham. He was deprived of the Great Seal in 1625 and later was heavily fined and imprisoned but, when released in 1640, proved a wise and loyal adviser to Charles I. It is believed by some historians that the Civil War might have been averted if the king had taken his advice. He was imprisoned by the Parliamentarians in 1641 but the next year, on his release, actively supported the king and became Archbishop of York. He died in 1650.

Conwy Castle has had a chequered history and became roofless after the Civil War, but even in ruin it created enthusiasm in most sightseers, who thought it more 'elegant' than Caernarfon. It was painted and described admiringly by all but Dr. Johnson, who was presumably becoming bored with sightseeing for he says that it ' . . . afforded nothing new. It is larger than that of Beaumaris, and less than that of Caernarfon . . . It is built on a rock so high and steep, that it is even now very difficult of access.'

It is to be regretted that the tubular railway bridge hides Telford's graceful suspension bridge on the landward side, and there is so much traffic on the new road bridge across the estuary of the Conwy that it is now impossible to see it properly from the seaward side. It must be admitted, however, that the castle may well owe its survival to the old London and North Western Railway which carried out the first restoration work to strengthen the towers against possible subsidence.

The parish church of Gyffin, now within the Conwy boundaries, has a carefully restored 15th century barrel ceiling over the altar, with 16 panels on which are painted the figures of saints. Bishop Richard Davies, scholar and Biblical translator, was born at Gyffin in 1501, and John Gibson was born there in 1790. Gibson moved to Liverpool with his parents when he was nine years old. His most famous sculpture is 'The Tinted Venus', which was exhibited at the Great Exhibition of 1862.

Conwy has been chosen as the northern terminus of the proposed Cambrian Way Footpath from Cardiff.

CRICIETH spreads around two wide bays separated by the little headland crowned by Cricieth castle. It has a delightful central green sloping down to the sea.

The castle was built by the Welsh princes in the 13th century and has interesting differences from the later Edwardian castles. In 1239 it was used as a prison for Gruffydd, the rebellious son of Llywelyn the Great. It faces and complements Harlech castle, ten miles away across Tremadog Bay. Although smaller, it held out stoutly in all the Welsh rebellions.

After his conquest of Wales Edward I stayed there on several occasions, and after his last visit, in 1284, he granted Cricieth a Charter. The Constables of the castle were also mayors, the most famous of whom was Sir Hywel y Fwyall (Howell of the Battle Axe), who had served under the Black Prince in the French Wars. Life in the castle in his time is vividly described in a poem by Iolo Goch.

Owain Glyndŵr inflicted considerable damage to the castle and the town, and in Elizabethan times Leland reported that there were only two or three houses, and the town 'clene decayed'. However, it retained its Borough status until 1873. Near the castle gate is Y Gegin, a small theatre gallery where exhibitions of great local interest are shown during the summer.

The town's development in the Victorian era left it a very pleasant place. Among the growing number of visitors was Rider Haggard, who refers to Black Rock, at the east end of the great beach, in his novel *Beatrice*, which he wrote when staying in Cricieth.

Brynawelon, the house David Lloyd George built before the first World War, which became the home of his daughter, Lady Megan Lloyd George, after his death, is on a hill north of the High Street.

Llanystumdwy, where Lloyd George spent his boyhood and where he is buried beside the Afon Dwyfor, from which he took his title, is 1½ miles west of Cricieth. The strikingly original memorial and the Lloyd George Museum were designed by Sir Clough Williams-Ellis. The beautifully arranged Museum displays the Deeds of Freedom, magnificent caskets, documents and other relics of the great statesman.

The Baptist Capel-y-Beirdd is named in honour of two natives of Llanystumdwy and has a memorial tablet to Robert Williams (Robert ap Gwilym Ddu: 1766-1850), author of many popular hymns, and David Owen (Dewi Wyn o Eifion: 1784-1841) who was a master of the strict metres.

West of Llanystumdwy, on the B.4354, is the little village of Chwilog, birthplace of John Thomas (Sion Wyn o Eifion), known as 'Bardd yn ei Wely' (the bard in his bed), who was confined to his bed at the age of 15, as the result of an accident, and remained there almost uninterruptedly until his death in 1859 at the age of 72. He seems to have been a most delightful character who never complained but busied himself with his studies. He taught himself English, played the flageolet and composed hymns. He was visited by Shelley, Richard Fenton, the Welsh historian, and other distinguished people.

Eliseus Williams (Eifion Wyn), who wrote in both the classical and the free metres, was born at Porthmadog, and is buried in Chwilog cemetery.

In one of the byways south-west of Chwilog is Penarth Fawr Medieval Hall, believed to have been built in 1416. Although it has undergone some alterations, including the insertion of a floor to form an upper storey, and the demolition of the northern end shortly after Pennant visited it in 1791, many of the original features remain. The buttery and pantry end is virtually in its original form.

East of Cricieth is Ynscynhaearn church. David Owen

the harpist, who died in 1741 and is buried in the churchyard, composed several well-known airs, the most famous of which is *Dafydd y Garreg Wen* (David of the White Rock), for which Sir Walter Scott wrote *The Dying Bard*, a reference to the tradition that the tune was composed by Dafydd on his death bed.

On a hill south-east of Cricieth is Treflys church, which has a 6th century stone bearing the Chi Rho monogram. There is only one other in Wales and seven in the whole of Britain.

DEGANNWY, on the Creuddyn Peninsula, is now within the boundaries of Conwy. Only slight traces of its historic castle remain, but it has the advantage of an incomparable view of the towers and walls of Conwy town and castle, backed by wooded hills, across the wide estuary of the Afon Conwy.

Maelgwyn Gwynedd kept his court at Dinas Conwy in the 6th century and several attempted invasions of Gwynedd by Saxons and Normans were halted there, both before and after the Normans built a timber castle on the Fardre, a hill behind the town. Henry III replaced the timber castle with one of stone in 1245 but only 19 years later it was in the hands of Prince Madog, and Edward I had the indignity of being besieged in Conwy Castle. His provisions were cut off and he was forced to live on salted meat and water sweetened with honey until the flooded river fell suddenly and he was able to cut off supplies to the attackers. They fled to Eryri, leaving the king and his men to have a belated Christmas feast of thanksgiving. Degannwy's castle was finally destroyed by Llywelyn the Last in 1263 and never rebuilt.

DINAS DINLLE, five miles south-west of Caernarfon, off the A.499, has been somewhat overrun by bungalows bordering the sandy beach but has the remains of an earthwork crowning a mound beside the sea. It dates from about 100 B.C. and commands a view of Yr Eifl on the Lleyn. A mile inland is Llandwrog where the church, although rebuilt in 1860, has some fine 18th century Wynne monuments.

Further north, west of the A.487, is the isolated little church of Llanfaglan, beside the Menai Strait. It has two grave slabs dating from the 11th or 12th century, and a 5th or early 6th century A.D. pillar-stone with a Latin inscription.

DOLWYDDELAN, on the A.470, in the wooded valley of the Lledr, was formerly a quarrymen's village. The castle was built about 1170 and is said to have been the birth-place of Llywelyn the Great. It stands commandingly on a precipitous rock and, although ruinous, is of interest for the use of slate slabs in the fireplace, roof and battlements, and some of the windows.

The original church was on Bryn y Bedd, on the south of the village, but was so hemmed in with trees that the congregation was in constant danger of surprise attacks. The present church was built in the 15th century and is one of the most interesting in the district. It is almost unaltered and is one of the few surviving examples of a carreg-mwysog (moss-stone) roof. The slates were laid on a bed of spagnum moss to prevent rain leaking through, a method which replaced the older thatched roofs in the 14th century.

The interior has a fine 15th century wooden screen surmounted by an 18th century wooden balustrade, some beautiful fragments of 16th century glass, much 18th century woodwork, one of the few brasses in Wales, depicting the kneeling figure of Maredudd ab Ieuan, who died in 1525, several Wynn memorials, including an elaborate Jacobean monument, and a transept added by Robert Wynn of Plas Mawr, Conwy.

Farther up the valley are fine views of Moel Siabod and Snowdon.

LLANAELHAEARN is on the B.4417, at the foot of Yr Eifl (The Three Forks, known to the English as The Rivals). The villages, like so many others now, was becoming depopulated, but instead of fatalistically accepting the change the little community determined to combat it. Under the inspiration of the local doctor they formed a co-operative venture. The share holders are all those on the electoral register and their enterprise covers all aspects of community life, including the local shop and post office and the village hall, with the happiest results which others with similar problems would do well to study.

The restored 12th century cruciform church has a 16th century rood-screen, spindle-backed box pews and two 5th or early 6th century inscribed stones.

The central peak of Yr Eifl drops down to the sea from a height of 1,849 ft. and on the summit is Tre'r Ceiri, an Iron Age encampment of more than 100 hut circles which vary in size from cell-like structures to circles 16ft. across. It appears to have been occupied as late as 400 A.D. On a clear day there is a magnificent view of the west coast of Wales from St. David's Head to Bangor, away to Holyhead Mountain in Anglesey and the whole of Snowdonia.

The district is associated with legends of the Welsh prince Vortigern, who so disastrously invited the Saxons, Hengist and Horsa, to his aid. His fabulous castle, which was destroyed 'by fire from heaven', is said to have been in the Nant Gwrtheyrn, a ravine running down from the peak.

LLANBERIS, in the north-west of the Snowdonia National Park, at the entrance to the Llanberis Pass, the wildest and most impressive in the area, is the nearest village to Snowdon (Yr Wyddfa). Old Llanberis, at the south-eastern end of Llyn Peris, close to the entrance to the Pass, is still little more than a mountain hamlet, with a 14th century church to which three aisles were added in the early 16th century. The medieval screen, with a small almsbox hollowed out of the side, has been restored. There is slate everywhere in the village, including slate tombstones with Welsh inscriptions.

The new village of Llanberis grew up on the south-eastern shore of Llyn Padarn to provide accommodation for the quarrymen.

The two lakes are connected by a short stream which is spanned by Pen-y-llan Bridge, a vantage point for wonderful views over both the mountain-cradled lakes. Dolbadarn Castle, on a spit of land jutting out into Llyn Peris, with Snowdon rising behind it, has a romantically beautiful setting. Llywelyn the Great imprisoned his brother Owain the Red there for 23 years, and Owain Glyndŵr imprisoned Lord Gray of Ruthin there in 1401.

The station for the Snowdon Railway, the only rack railway in England and Wales, is west of the bridge. Opened in 1896, it has a gauge of 2ft. 7½ins., with a rack rail in the centre, and has locomotives made in the Swiss locomotive works at Winterthur. It climbs 3,560 ft. to the top of Snowdon, where there is the highest station in England and Wales. If the weather is clear, there is a superb and wide-spreading view from the summit. The waterfall of Nant Ceunant, east of the railway, is a fine sight after heavy rain.

Llanberis is also the starting point for the easiest of the numerous paths to the summit. Other ascents of varying difficulty can be made by the Miners' Track, at the top of Llanberis Pass, the Pyg Track, from near Penygwryd, from the south at Nant Gwynant, and on the west from Rhyd-Ddu, a small quarrymen's village which was the birthplace of the distinguished Welsh poets and men of letters, R.Williams-Parry and his cousin, Sir Thomas Parry-Williams.

The famous Horseshoe, which has been called the finest ridge walk in Europe, is essentially one of the routes which are not for the beginner and like most of the ascents, should only be attempted after expert advice has been given, and with due regard for the weather. Thick mists can sweep down on Snowdon with terrifying abruptness and all too often have disastrous consequences for the inexperienced. They can provide an uncomfortable experience for even the most expert.

The Llanberis Lake Railway has been laid out on the track of the old slate quarry railway, along the eastern shore of Llyn Padarn. The single track line is two miles long, with a gauge of 1ft. 11½ins., and is steam operated. The North Wales Quarrying Museum, in the former workshops of the Dinorwic Slate quarry at Gilfach Ddu, has much of the original machinery, including a 50ft. waterwheel. The quarry, which was worked from 1809 until it closed in 1969, rises in step-like terraces for 1,800 ft. above Llyn Peris.

Bryn Bras castle, south of the A.4080, 3½ miles north-west of Llanberis, was built in the 1830's. It has beautifully laid out grounds with woodland walks, waterfalls, pools and fine views.

LLANDUDNO, on the Creuddyn Peninsula, sheltered by Great and Little Orme, is a perfect example of a Victorian holiday resort which has been imaginatively adapted to the present day. It is the largest and most popular seaside town and conference centre in Gwynedd. It was laid out by Lord Mostyn in 1849 between two bays, one facing north and the other facing west, both of which command extensive views of the north coast and Snowdonia.

Llandudno also has all the appurtenances demanded of a popular resort, including a fine pier and pavilion, and its long, level streets and promenade are so wide that even in the height of the season traffic flows well and there is ample room for pedestrians to stroll at ease, particularly in Gloddaeth Avenue, the great boulevard which links the two beaches.

The most recent of Llandudno's attractions is the Doll Museum, which has over 1,000 dolls from all parts of the world, including many in costume - some very primitive and others exquisitely dressed, including a 19th century French fashion doll. There is also a small collection of model railways.

Although Llandudno has no history, the district around has many prehistoric relics, ancient churches and fine old mansions. On the summit of Great Orme is the little church founded by St.Tudno, a 7th century anchorite, a cromlech, a rocking stone, copper mines worked by the Romans and the site of a British encampment. The Great Orme Nature Trail starts from the Happy Valley, and the summit can also be reached by the Marine Drive or by the little cable railway opened in 1902. The latter has a gauge of 3ft. 6½ins., and a maximum gradient of 1 in 3½.

There are only scanty remains of Gogarth Abbey, which was in ruins when Leland visited it in the reign of Henry VIII.

Penmorfa, now the Gogarth Abbey Hotel, on the West Shore, was the summer home of Dean Liddell, whose little daughter was the original 'Alice' of Lewis Carroll's *Alice in Wonderland*. Lewis Carroll frequently visited the family and revised the book for a second edition whilst staying there. A memorial on the sea-shore, depicting a White Rabbit consulting his watch, was erected in 1933.

Gloddaeth Hall, the home of the Mostyn family from about 1458, was once famous for the breeding of house-doves which are mentioned in Letter XL1V, addressed to Pennant, in White's *The Natural History of Selborne*. Parts of Gloddaeth date from 1584, and it has a magnificent Great Hall in which Elizabeth I, Queen Victoria and 'Carmen Sylva', Queen of Rumania, have been entertained. Once one of the most celebrated centres of Welsh culture, it is now an English school.

Bodysgallen, the ancient seat of the Mostyns, came into the possession of the Wynn family before 1594 when Hugh Wynn married the sole heiress of Richard Mostyn of Bodysgallen, a man of great learning especially noted for his love of Welsh literature. It is now a private hotel. There are memorials of the Wynn and Mostyn families in the restored Llanrhos church.

LLANFAIRFECHAN, on the north coast between Aber and Penmaenmawr, is a scattered little town with the older part half a mile inland, in a steep wooded combe of the hills, and the newer houses along the A.55, which bridges a cheerful little tree-fringed mountain stream dropping 2,000ft. in three miles on its dash to the sea.

The pleasantly unpretentious esplanade commands wide views across the Menai Strait to south-east Anglesey and Ynys Seiriol. Christ Church dates from 1855. It has one of the finest organs in North Wales and organ recitals are given on Sunday evenings during the summer season. The parish church of St. Mary's holds its evening services in Welsh.

The Snowdonia Stone Art Gallery in Mill Road has an unusual permanent display of commemorative slate pictures with replicas in slate of stamps, flags and various interesting events.

LLANGELYNIN has a remote little church on a steep hill, 927ft. above sea level, on hills west of the Afon Conwy, and is claimed to be one of the highest-sited parish churches in Wales.

Founded by St. Celynin in the 7th century, it has a simple dignity of its own. The nave dates back to the 11th or 12th century and there are a late 14th century chancel, a fine 15th century east window, porch and transept, a wooden barrel roof and remnants of an oak screen. There is also a bench dated 1629 and a font of unknown origin. Until some time in the 19th century the women worshipped in the 12ft. wide nave and the men in the raised north transept, known as Capel-y-Meibion (Men's Chapel), which still has its original earthen floor.

Ffynnon Gelynin, in the churchyard, was once used for divination. The clothes of sick children were placed on the water: if they floated, the child would recover, but if they sank, it would die.

LLANRHYCHWYN church, known as Llywelyn's Old Church, is 1½ miles north-west of Llanrwst. It was the mother church of Trefriw and of Betws-y-Coed. It is strikingly set on a rock among lonely hills and is surrounded by a high stone wall. The roof is of beautifully graduated slating, now rare, and its old ridging is intact.

Llywelyn the Great and his wife worshipped in the church until he built Trefriw church, closer to one of his palaces, in 1230 'for the ease of his Princess, who before was obliged to go on foot to Llanrhychwyn'. The south aisle is the oldest part of the church, with thick walls and heavy beams. The north aisle was added in the 16th century. There is a very ancient, small, square font, stained glass depicting a Trinity in brown line and yellow stain of about 1460 which is probably the earliest example of stained glass in the locality; also a fine old bell, which may have come from Maenan Abbey, and a pulpit dated 1691.

Robert Williams (Trebor Mai), one of the most famous englynion writers of the 19th century, was born at Llanrhychwyn. Many of his englynion (four line alliterative stanzas) are still among the best in the Welsh language.

LLANRWST, in the Conwy Valley, was in Denbighshire until the administrative changes of 1974. It is the market town and shopping centre of the Upper Conwy Valley. Set beside the river in lush meadows, it has two notable possessions - the graceful three-arched bridge across the river, traditionally designed by Inigo Jones for his friend, Sir Richard Wynn of Gwydir, and the parish church, with the superb Gwydir chapel. The church was built in 1470 on an earlier site. The richly carved rood-screen and rood-loft are the finest in the district and of an individualistic Welsh character, each of the pointed arches being filled with a different design. It is believed to have been brought from Maenan Abbey at the Dissolution. The site of the abbey is 2 miles north of Llanrwst.

The Gwydir Chapel, which was added to the church in 1633, has been restored with the help of the Pilgrim Trust. It has carved screens, stalls and panelling and an elaborate oak roof, also said to have come from Maenan Abbey. The remarkable range of monuments includes a huge empty stone coffin, believed to have been that of Llywelyn the Great. The finest of the six beautifully engraved portrait brasses commemorates Sarah Wynn, who died in 1671. There are also a quaint little effigy of Sidney Wynn, who died in 1639 at the age of one month, and relics of the half legendary exploits of Dafydd ap Siencyn, 'The Welsh Robin Hood', who supported the Lancastrian cause in the Wars of the Roses, and of Hywel Coetmor, who fought at Poitiers and owned Gwydir before it was bought by the Wynns in the 16th century.

Almshouses founded in 1610 flank the entrance to the churchyard. Harps engraved on some of the gravestones are a reminder that Llanrwst was once famous for its harp-makers.

English visitors first 'discovered' Llanrwst in the 19th century. Macaulay stayed there in 1821, with a reading party, and he and his friends received a testimonial signed by 25 townsmen in appreciation of their 'good conduct, demeanour and public spirit'.

Llanrwst was also a great intellectual centre and there is a long list of poets and preachers born in the town and its neighbourhood, many of whom were educated at the Grammar School founded by Sir John Wynn in the 17th century as a free school. The slight remains of Plas Isaf, the ancestral home of William Salesbury, chief translator of the first Welsh New Testament, are near the station.

Encounter, the North Wales Museum of Wild Life, has big game trophies and stuffed birds, collected before the days of the more humane telephoto camera lens came into its own. There are also exhibits of wild life in Snowdonia and a collection of rare birds from the South Pacific.

Tu Hwnt I'r Bont (The House Beyond the Bridge), at the west end of the bridge across the Conwy, is a 15th century stone building which was originally used as a court house. It now belongs to the National Trust and has teas, Welsh woollens, pottery, prints and books for sale.

Gwydir Castle (more correctly Gwedir), half a mile from Llanrwst at the junction of the Llanrwst, Betws-y-coed and Conwy Roads, is an historic mansion built by the Wynns in the 16th century. It was badly damaged by fire in 1912 and 1922 but has been partly restored. There are many tropical birds, peacocks and clipped yew trees in the grounds, which are beautifully laid out. On the opposite side of the road is a steep path through woods leading to Gwydir Uchaf, the Dower House, now a district office of the Forestry Commission. It has an interesting little 17th century chapel with its original fittings and a curious painted ceiling.

Farther north, on the B.5106 to Conwy, is Trefriw, on the banks of the Afon Crafnant, a tributary of the Afon Conwy. It is a pleasant village along the wooded foothills of the great range rising to the Carnedds. It is at the highest navigable point of the Conwy and there are trips up and down the river during the summer.

Llywelyn the Great had a palace at Trefriw, of which no trace remains, and the church he founded to save his princess the tiring uphill walk to the Old Church at Llanrhychwyn has been too greatly altered to bear much resemblance to the original buildings.

The once famous spa is 1½ miles north of the village. It has been re-opened recently and is said to have the richest sulphur-iron waters in the world.

Still farther north along the same road is Dolgarrog, with its falls, houses climbing the wooded slopes, and the uncluttered lines of the Hydro-Electric Power Works;

also Tal-y-bont, a summer haunt of artists, and Caerhun, with an unpretentious village church which has a double bell-cot but only one bell. Caerhun stands within the ramparts of the Roman station of Canovium, where two Roman roads met, but little now remains of interest.

NEFYN is the largest of the sea-side resorts on the north coast of Lleyn, although it has a population of only 2,000 or so. It is on cliffs above sandy beaches which reach from the western shoulder of Yr Eifl to Morfa Nefyn and the peninsula of Porth Dinllaen, and looks north across Caernarfon Bay. The old church of St. Mary's was rebuilt in the 1820's and has a narrow tower topped by a disproportionately large weather vane in the form of a ship.

The remains of prehistoric fortresses and cromlechau can be found on some of the neighbouring hills, and the whole area abounds in legends and more dependable historical associations. Giraldus Cambrensis found at Nefyn a Welsh copy of *The Prophesies of Merlin*, for which he had been searching, and Edward I held a tournament there in 1284 in imitation of King Arthur and the Round Table. The Black Prince bestowed Nefyn upon Nigel de Loring in 1355 for his services in Gascony and it was created a free borough, with two fairs annually and a weekly market. It retained its corporate unity until 1883 and still treasures the original charter, a silver seal, and other relics of its former status.

Morfa Nefyn, a mile west of Nefyn, has the natural harbour of Porth Dinllaen, which was an important shipping centre until Holyhead harbour was opened in 1873.

The B.4412 from Morfa Nefyn joins the A.497 from Nefyn to cut straight across the peninsula to the railway station at Pwllheli, passing the 18th century mansion of Bodegroes, surrounded by woods through which a public road runs, and Bodfel Hall, in which Mrs. Thrale was born. She visited it in 1744 with her husband and Dr.

Johnson, who was not feeling well. He says 'Mrs. Thrale remembered the rooms, and wandered over them with recollections of her childhood. This species of pleasure is always melancholy. The walk was cut down and the pond was dry . . . '.

PENMACHNO, on the eastern borders of Snowdonia, 3½ miles from Betws-y-coed on the B.446, is a quarrymen's village in Cwm Machno.

Iorwerth, father of Llywelyn the Great, is said to have been buried in an earlier church on the site. The present church has two panels of an early 16th century oak triptych, painted on both sides, which was given to the church in 1713, and three early Christian monuments, two of which have inscriptions of special interest. One uses the Celtic 'Venedos' referring to Welsh 'Gwynedd', showing that the north-west area of Wales was separately identified as early as the late 5th or early 6th century. It also has the only known instance of the use in Britain of the terms *civis* and *magistratus* on an early Christian inscription, implying the existence of an ordered system of government in the area even after the departure of the Romans. The inscription on the other stone says it was set up 'in the time of Justinius the Consul'. He was consul in A.D. 540 and was one of the two last Roman consuls cited on monuments in the Western World.

There is also a memorial window to Bishop William Morgan, the first translator of the entire Bible into Welsh. It standardized and stabilized the Welsh language at a time when it was in danger of being superseded by English.

Bishop Morgan was born in the parish in 1541, at Tŷ Mawr, in the Gwynant Valley. The stone-built farmhouse of Tŷ Mawr now belongs to the National Trust.

PENMAENMAWR, on the north coast, in a fertile, sheltered valley between the great headlands of Penmaenmawr and Penmaenbach and backed by an amphitheatre of mountains, grew up in the 19th century. It is as much loved by families on holiday to-day as it was by the Victorians. A bronze bust at the head of the road linking the town centre and the sea front commemorates W.E. Gladstone, who stayed annually for many years at 'dear old Penmaenmawr'. Another appreciative visitor was Sir Edward Elgar, who completed the full score of *Falstaff* at a house called Tan-yr-allt.

In earlier times travellers were forced to cross the formidable 1,300 ft. high Penmaenmawr Mountain, which rises almost perpendicularly from the sea. Many preferred to drive or walk across the vast Lavan Sands which reach away from Penmaenmawr nearly to Beaumaris. Even this could be dangerous, and in foggy weather a bell was rung from Llanfairfechan church for their guidance. A new and safer road was constructed in 1772 by tunnelling through Penmaenmawr and Penmaenbach, with a strong wall protecting those stretches of the road which did not pass through the tunnels.

There is a pretty Dingle just off the main street of Penmaenmawr, a wooded 'Fairy Glen' with a waterfall beside the road, and a superb drive over the great Sychnant Pass. The road rises 300 ft. in a mile and has a descent of 1 in 7½. A History Trail has been planned to include the 'Druid Circle' on Graig Lwyd, 1,200 ft. above sea level, and the site of an important Stone Age factory where many hundreds of axes in various stages of manufacture have been found. There is evidence that trade was carried on with even the most distant parts of Britain.

PENRHYN CASTLE is 1½ miles south-east of Bangor at the junction of the A.5 and A.55. The great battlemented gateway and enormously high walls along the road hide the granite pile built for the first Lord Penrhyn between 1827 and 1840. It is now in the care of the National Trust. Much of the Victorian furniture, some of which is in the 'Norman' style, a slate bedstead and paintings remain, and the whole effect is rather overwhelming. There is also an Industrial Railway Museum in the stables, a collection of over 1,000 dolls, a natural history display and a pottery in the grounds. The Victorian garden with its formal bedding contrasts with the beautiful park, which covers 700 acres and in which are many exotic trees and shrubs.

Llandegai, beside the main entrance, is a model village built by Lord Penrhyn. The church was founded by St. Tegai in the late 6th century but was rebuilt in the 16th century. It is approached through a fine avenue of yew trees and has a monument brought there from Llanfaes Priory after the Dissolution, 15th century alabaster tombs and the kneeling figure of John Williams, Archbishop of York. He was descended from the Gruffydds of Penrhyn and the Williams family of Cochwillan Hall, in the Ogwen Valley. Penrhyn had been sold to buy a pardon for Prŷs Gruffydd, an Elizabethan 'sea-dog' of whom many stories are told, but the Archbishop bought back the property at the height of his career. Cochwillan was sold in 1620, and only the Great Hall, now used as a barn, remains.

There is also a monument in Llandegai church by Westmacott to the first Lord and Lady Penrhyn, with the mourning figures of a quarryman and of Hope.

PORT DINORWIC, or Y FELINHELI, is midway along the shore of the Menai Strait, between Bangor and Caernarfon, on the mainland side of the ancient ferry to Moel-y-Don in Anglesey. The road to Bangor skirts the long wall of Vaynol Park, the seat of the Williams family in the 16th century and afterwards inherited by Thomas Assheton-Smith, the famous sportsman, who was M.P. for Caernarfonshire from 1832 to 1841. It was he who developed the Dinorwic Slate quarries and built the Llanberis Hotel and the narrow-gauge railway to convey slates from Llanberis to Port Dinorwic, but he is better remembered as the Master of the Quorn, and subsequently of the Burton Hounds and other packs, and as a cricketer and yachtsman. The harbour at Dinorwic is now a very popular and crowded Marina.

PORTHMADOG and TREMADOG, on the north of the Glaslyn estuary, owe their existence to the enterprise of one man, A.W. Madocks, son of John Madocks of Fron Yw, Denbighshire, from whom he inherited a great fortune.

Madocks built himself a house, Tanrallt, in 1800 - said to have been the first Regency house built in Wales - and laid out Tremadog in 1806 around a central square. It is still an unspoiled example of a Regency town, with a Town Hall (now a Crafts Centre), an hotel, a theatre (now a chapel) and a small Gothic church.

Shelley rented a house in the grounds of Tanrallt (since demolished) between 1812 and 1813, and wrote at least part of *Queen Mab* there.

A plaque on the Christian Mountain Centre, formerly a private house known as Woodlands, commemorates the birth there in 1888 of T.E. Lawrence (Lawrence of Arabia).

The old parish church, south of Penmorfa, has memories of Sir John Owen of Clenennau, the Welsh royalist, and his wife, and of the Huddart family of Brynkir. Clenennau, now a farmhouse, is 2 miles from Penmorfa. Brynkir Hall, a mile up the peaceful, wooded Cwm Pennant, with its curious Victorian tower half-hidden by trees, is now ruinous and said to be haunted.

The single long street from which Porthmadog grew was not begun until the mid-19th century, when trade had developed and some 50,000 tons of slates were being shipped annually from the new harbour. It is now the larger of the two resorts.

It was at Porthmadog that Lloyd George set up as a solicitor and laid the foundations of his fame in the

Llanfrothen burial case when he won the right for a Nonconformist to be buried in the churchyard with a service by a minister of his own denomination, which the then Vicar of Llanfrothen had refused.

Madock's whole enterprise arose when he read in Pennant's Tours an account of the ideas of Sir John Wynn of Gwydir for enclosing the Traeth Mawr. He bought the Tanrallt Estate, Penmorfa, and enclosed 1,000 acres of the Traeth Mawr. Then he obtained an Act of Parliament to enclose another 3,000 acres and began building an embankment, locally known as The Cob, across the Glaslyn Estuary. This first embankment was badly damaged in 1812 in a storm but a second was built successfully as the result of an appeal, which was supported enthusiastically by Shelley who headed the list of subscribers with a donation of £100.

Thomas Love Peacock lamented the loss of the waters of the estuary, which had formerly reflected the mountains, but the embankment is still the finest of all viewpoints from which to see the Snowdon range. It also commands a view of Lleyn and southward to the mountains of Meirionydd - a view so majestic that when a power line was constructed across the estuary, it was buried underground at a cost of two million pounds. It is to be regretted that modern holiday flats have since been built which strike a discordant note.

Tremadog and Porthmadog were named after their founder but also commemorate the persistent tradition that the Welsh Prince Madog ab Owain Gwynedd set sail from the Glaslyn estuary in the 12th century and discovered America. The belief has given rise to several explorations down the centuries in search of a tribe of Indians, said to be the Welsh-speaking descendants of Madog and his men. The story also formed the basis of Southey's narrative poem *Madoc*.

Madocks also planned a railway along The Cob which was eventually incorporated by Act of Parliament in 1832. After three years of very hard work, it conveyed its first load of slates in 1836. The engineer, James Spooner, ensured as far as was practicable a uniform falling gradient to enable slate trains to run down to the sea from Blaenau Ffestiniog by gravity, motive power being needed only to return the empties. This involved considerable feats of engineering and many problems were overcome, as the line rises 700 ft. in its 14-mile climb through the Moelwyn Mountains, yet the ascent is nowhere steeper than 1 in 79.

Spooner later advocated steam power to deal with the increasing traffic, but the proposal raised a storm of controversy. Many, including Robert Stephenson, thought it impracticable to use steam locomotives on a gauge of only 1 ft. 11½ ins. After James Spooner's death his son, Charles E. Spooner, went ahead and in 1863 ordered two locomotives which proved capable of hauling as many as 60 empty slate wagons up the gradients to Blaenau Ffestiniog.

It was on the Ffestiniog Railway that C.E. Spooner experimented with his first Fairlie locomotive in 1869. Alexander II of Russia sent observers to watch the trials and engineers came from all over the world. As a result many Fairlie locomotives were built for mountainous regions in various parts of the world, particularly South America and India. The first British bogie coach, built in 1873, was originally run on the Ffestiniog line.

The passenger service on the Ffestiniog Railway was suspended in 1940, and I still remember my dismay when in 1945 I saw the well-loved little coaches rotting away at Porthmadog. All services ceased the following year. Luckily a devoted band of railway enthusiasts began operating it again in 1954. The historic little engines now in use include two Fairlie locomotives, made in the Ffestiniog Railway workshops, which are believed to be the only examples of the type still running. The train now has a licensed buffet car serving light refreshments and ices.

On 28th May, 1969, the Ffestiniog Railway

reintroduced the Railway Letter Service by which, on payment of a fee, letters may be sent by rail, or by railway and G.P.O., especially franked at the stations on the railway. Commemorative covers and stamps depicting the Fairlie engine were issued in 1969.

The Ffestiniog Railway Museum at Porthmadog has a small collection of relics of the old days of the railway. The *Garlandstone*, a sailing ketch which first visited Porthmadog in 1909, is now moored alongside the reconstructed 19th century slate wharf of Porthmadog harbour. There is an interesting Maritime Museum in the cargo hold, with relics of the town's maritime past and of the ships built there.

Borth-y-gest, half a mile south of Porthmadog, is a pretty 19th century village set around a beautiful sandy bay, but the long beach of the neighbouring Morfa Bychan is now cluttered with caravans.

North of Porthmadog is Pont Croesor which carries the B.4410 across the Afon Glaslyn to Llanfrothen. The simple little isolated church has 13th century lancet windows at the east end, an oak chancel screen and a chest hollowed from a tree trunk.

Near Llanfrothen church is the arched gatehouse of Plas Brondanw, the home of the Williams-Ellis family. The 17th century house was rebuilt by Sir Clough Williams-Ellis in the 1950's after a fire. It can be glimpsed from the lane leading to Croesor, at the head of the lonely Cwm Croesor dominated by Cnicht. It was here that the late Bob Owen Croesor, as he was affectionately known to many, lived and amassed his collection of Welsh books and manuscripts, now in the National Library of Wales.

Six miles north of Porthmadog is the entrance to the well-wooded Aberglaslyn Pass, 400 acres of which are now in the care of the National Trust. Before the embankment was built at Porthmadog small ships sailed up as far as Pont Aberglaslyn, now celebrated for its view.

The Welsh Highland Railway, which shared the Ffestiniog's Porthmadog station, originated in 1877 as the North Wales Narrow Gauge Railway between Dinas Junction and Beddgelert. It had a gauge of 1 ft. 11½ ins. When its name was changed in 1922 it was extended through the pass of Aberglaslyn to Porthmadog, but two of the engines had to have their chimneys, domes and cabs cut down to enable them to pass through the Aberglaslyn tunnels. Between South Snowdon Station and Beddgelert the line followed the same route as that described by George Borrow in *Wild Wales*. The line was closed in 1936 but there are many who remember the smiling Stationmistress who dispensed refreshments at Beddgelert.

A Welsh Highland Railway Preservation Society was formed in 1964. The members are now actively engaged in rebuilding the railway, land has been bought for a new terminal at Porthmadog, and early locomotives and other rolling stock have been acquired.

P WLLHELI is set on Cardigan Bay at the point where the Lleyn joins the main body of Caernarfonshire and commands a panorama of coast and mountains extending for over 50 miles.

The older part of the town is close under the hills, with the newer holiday area of 'West End' beside the vast beach where a breezy expanse of grass-grown sand-dunes curves protectingly around the natural harbour which covers about 100 acres.

Pwllheli was given by Edward, the Black Prince, to his companion-in-arms, Sir Nigel Loring, at the same time as Nefyn, and was granted permission for a weekly market and two annual 'Hiring Fairs'. The citizens of Pwllheli had to pay their new lord £14 a year - a large sum of money in those days - while Sir Nigel paid the Crown an annual token rent of a single rose!

Pwllheli still possesses the original matrix of the Seal, on which the name is spelt 'Porthely', but the ancient parish church was rebuilt in 1887 and no buildings remain - nor is there any record of any building of great importance. In 1821 *The Cambrian Tourist*, remarking on its 'excellent beach', said 'it appears probable it will grow into notice as a sea-bathing resort', but 30 years later, in spite of its obvious potentialities, it was still noted chiefly for its large weekly markets, its ship-building industry and its coastal trade.

Pwllheli's development as a holiday centre came when it was chosen as the most northerly terminus of the old Cambrian Railway, now part of British Rail (W.R.). It is still 'The Gateway to the Lleyn' and its nearest railhead. It is an area abounding in prehistoric relics, fascinating legends and historical associations with Welsh and English events.

Although the huge Butlin's Holiday Camp is only four miles to the east, Pwllheli remains as Welsh as its name.

Abererch, a mile north-east of Pwllheli, is just off the A.499 main Pwllheli-Caernarfon Road which skirts Yr Eifl on the north coast of Lleyn. It is a secluded little village, gay in summer with masses of hydrangeas in the cottage gardens. Its restored medieval church has some 15th century misericordes and poppy-heads. It faces the red and white Ebenezer Chapel at the top of a hill above the River Erch.

Abererch is on the edge of the wide beach of Morfa Abererch, and just out to sea is a rock where families of seals can be seen. John Elias, the great Welsh preacher, whose work lay chiefly in Anglesey, was born at Abererch in 1774.

SNOWDONIA NATIONAL PARK, which came into

being in 1951, covers some 840 square miles of north-west Wales, all but a few square miles of which lie within Gwynedd. It extends from Penmaenmawr Mountain on the north coast, southward to the Dyfi estuary, and includes the whole of the Snowdon group, the Arans and Arenigs, Dduallt, Rhobell, Rhinog Fawr and Rhinog

Fach, Diffwys, Llethr and the Cadair Idris range.

The National Park area is not only one of great variety and beauty - of mountains, valleys, lakes, rivers, waterfalls and seacoast - but of ancient churches, castles, towns and mansions, thriving farms, busy villages and remote cottages, with a history reaching into the mists of antiquity and a wealth of literary associations. Living traditions of past customs, beliefs and ideals are wedded to an awareness of modern progress.

The people of Snowdonia have an inherent love of music and poetry, which gives rise to local and provincial eisteddfodau, and finds its culmination in the annual Royal National Eisteddford, held in North and South Wales in alternate years. Men and women from all over Wales compete, but the solo or choral pennillion singing - improvised singing to a harp - is the special inheritance of Gwynedd. The men who farm the fertile soil of the valleys and on the coastal plain have much in common with English farmers, but those who farm on the hills have an incredibly hard life, with small, uncertain returns; yet in the past it was seldom that a hill man would leave this incessant toil for the less arduous and more profitable lowland farms. To-day depopulation is posing many problems as the younger men and women seek the towns, and the abandoned farms and cottages are bought up as holiday homes and left untenanted for the greater part of the year.

Many of the once famous slate and granite quarries of North Wales have been closed and nowadays by far the larger number of people in the rural areas of the National Park are engaged in farming or forestry work, but there are also many woollen mills producing traditional Welsh designs, most of which are open to the public at stated times. There are also small service industries, lead mines and aluminium and hydro-electric works, but it has no great industrial areas, as the clear air testifies.

The geology of the National Park area is of the greatest interest and complexity, showing the oldest series of sedimentary rock, Pre-Cambrian azoic strata amidst igneous and eruptive rocks. The fauna includes the badger and the polecat and it is the only place where the pine marten survives in Southern Britain. The bird life is of great variety and many rare plants and flowers flourish in the remoter regions, particularly alpines.

The National Park also has ample provision for indoor and outdoor amusements and the largest number of narrow-gauge railways in Wales. All are now operated by enthusiastic members of various Preservation Societies.

The name 'Snowdonia' has passed into common usage and has been adopted as the name of the National Park, but in all early accounts, from the time of Giraldus Cambrensis onwards, the English name of Snowdon (Snow Mountain) applied to the whole region and not to a single mountain. It is believed that Thomas Pennant was the first to use the term 'Snowdonia'.

The old Welsh name, Eryri, long believed to mean 'the breeding place of eagles', has been traced by the great Welsh scholar, Sir Ifor Williams, to the *Black Book of Carmarthen*, a 13th century manuscript where it signifies a rise in the land and probably meant only 'the high mountain land'. The Welsh name for the highest peak is 'Yr Wyddfa', which means a tumulus or grave.

Such a striking and varied landscape with so many sources of enjoyment inevitably attracts great numbers of tourists and holiday makers, but a 'National Park' is not intended purely as a pleasure ground. It is an area where people live and work, as their ancestors have done for many generations. Making it a National Park effects no change in the ownership of the land and confers on the public no additional right of access to the countryside.

The Snowdonia National Park Committee tries to maintain a balance between those whose livelihood is gained in the valleys and on the mountainsides, and visitors, who should remember that the inhabitants have prior rights and that the Country Code must be observed, to avoid causing damage and even heavy losses through ignorance or thoughtlessness.

Large areas under the control of the Forestry Commission are Forest Parks and have forest walks laid out and picnic areas provided.

The National Park also has a number of National Nature Reserves which are the outdoor scientific laboratories of the Nature Conservancy. About seven and a half thousand acres of special interest to geologists and naturalists can be visited only by serious students, who have to obtain a special permit.

TUDWEILIOG, a hill-top village on the north coast of Lleyn, lies between the beach of Porth Ysgadan and Carn Fadrun, which rises 1,217 ft. and dominates western Lleyn. There is an important Iron Age hill-fort on the summit and some very interesting villages, churches and mansions in the neighbourhood.

The Thrales and Dr. Johnson visited the churches of Tudweiliog and Llangwynnadl, which Mrs. Thrale held 'by impropriation', and found them in a shocking state of disrepair.

Tudweiliog church was rebuilt by Sir Gilbert Scott in 1850, but the spacious church of Llangwynnadl, now beautifully kept like most churches in Lleyn, is little altered. It has three naves, each under a gabled arch, and an unusual carved inscription on the pillars which gives the date of building as 1520; also a 16th century communion cup and paten, and hassocks covered in various designs in *gros-point*. It once possessed a bronze handbell brought from Ireland in the 8th century. It was one of the few Celtic handbells surviving in Wales and is now in the National Museum of Wales at Cardiff.

Penllech, north of Llangwynnadl, straggles along the old Pilgrims' Way, or Saints' Road (B.4417), which leads to Aberdaron. There is a fine cromlech nearby on the slopes of Mynydd Cefnamlwch where thick woods hide the mansion which was the seat of the Griffith family from the 14th century until the estate passed by inheritance to the Wynne-Finch family of Foelas in the 18th century.

On the northern slopes of Carn Fadrun is the diminutive church of Llandudwen, with an octagonal font believed to date from the 10th century and one of the two pre-Reformation silver chalices to be found in Wales. Close by is Madryn Castle, once the seat of Sir Love-Jones-Parry, whose travels abroad in 1858 with his mother and fiancée, Miss Griffith, have been retold by Hugh J. Owen in *Sir Love's Adventures in Spain,* with notes from Miss Griffith's Diary. It reflects the stoicism needed by even the wealthiest travellers in Spain before the days of 'package' holidays. The old gatehouse of Madryn remains almost intact but the castle itself has been largely rebuilt.

Llaniestyn, on the south of Carn Fadrun, five miles from Tudweiliog, is in a sheltered valley with a beautiful old church which has a musicians' gallery.

Y SBYTY IFAN, on the B.4407, in the upper Conwy valley, is a quiet village set in wild mountain scenery. The area is part of the vast Penrhyn Estate owned by the National Trust and covers 40 sq. miles, most of it well over 1,500 ft. above sea level. Ysbyty Ifan derives its name from a hospice of the Knights of St. John of Jerusalem, of which Pennant says it was 'so styled from having formed in the then inhospitable country an asylum and guard for travellers under the protection of the knight who held the manor and made its precincts a sanctuary', but that after the abolition of the Order 'this privilege became the bane of the neighbourhood for the place thus exempted from all jurisdiction was converted into a den of thieves and murderers, who ravaged the country far and wide with impunity, till the reign of Henry VII, when they were extirpated by the bravery and prudence of Merdydd ab Evan'.

The church has been rebuilt on ancient foundations but has three recumbent alabaster effigies of the Rhys family of Plas Iolyn - Rhys ap Meredydd (Rhys Fawr), who fought at Bosworth with Henry Tudor (afterwards Henry VII), Lowry, Rhys's wife, and their son Sir Robert ap Rhys, who was cross-bearer and chaplain to Cardinal Wolsey. Sir Robert's son was Elis Prys (Y Doktor Coch: the Red Doctor), so called from the robes of his degree from Cambridge, who played a leading part in the destruction of Welsh monasteries at the Dissolution.

SIR FEIRIONYDD (MEIRIONYDD)

ABERDYFI (ABERDOVEY), a delightful little seaside resort on the southern boundary of the Snowdonia National Park, looks south across the beautiful Dyfi estuary which separates Gwynedd in North Wales from Dyfed in South Wales.

Aberdyfi was so remote in earlier times that although Llywelyn the Great held a Parliament there in 1216, which was virtually the first Welsh Parliament, no other events of importance seem to have taken place since.

In the 18th century it became a flourishing port with a busy ship-building yard, and Aberdyfi ships traded to the farthest corners of the earth. Their fascinating story is told in the Rev. D.W. Morgan's *Brief Glory*, and their traditions are carried on by the Outward Bound School for Boys. There is also an Outward Bound School for Girls. The little Outward Bound Sailing Museum exhibits models of sailing ships, sailors' navigation instruments, tools and ropework, including early Royal National Lifeboat Institution equipment.

There are some good Georgian houses and the Ship Inn (now re-named The Dovey) has a plaque saying it was built in 1792.

Aberdyfi and the whole of the Cambrian Coast of Cardigan Bay, from Aberystwyth to Pwllheli, were opened up with the coming of the Cambrian Railway, formed by the incorporation in 1864 of a number of smaller railways. I knew and loved the intensely Welsh character of all its ramification of branch lines.

The Cambrian Railway was absorbed by the Great Western Railway in 1921, and more recently most of its branch lines were closed under the Beeching Axe, including the finest of all through the Vale of Llangollen, but at least the old Aberystwyth line and the coastal railway to Pwllheli have survived. It is to be hoped they will remain open as long as railways last.

In the Victorian and Edwardian eras English visitors 'discovered' Aberdyfi and houses were terraced on the hills above the estuary to accommodate them. True to English tradition, an 18-hole championship golf course was laid out on the sand-dunes, the name of the rugged Cwm Dyffryn was changed to 'Happy Valley' and it became part of a 'Panorama walk' past Llyn Barfog, which became 'The Bearded Lake'. Llyn Barfog is one of many Welsh lakes with legends of fairies and their milk-white cattle and a greedy farmer who flies in the face of fortune.

Dibdin's song *The Bells of Aberdovey*, composed for the opera *Liberty Hall,* which was produced at Drury Lane in 1785, has carried the name of Aberdovey to many parts of the world, but it overlooks the fact that the church was not built until 1832 and before that the nearest church was at Tywyn, five miles to the north. The legend of a drowned city, on which the song was based, is yet another common along the Welsh coast and may be a folk memory of an inundation in prehistoric times.

There is a brass in Aberdyfi church to Baron James Richard Atkin, who was born in Australia in 1857. He is shown in his judge's robes as Lord of Appeal. His mother was a descendant of the Rucks of Pantlludw, near Pennal, an old-established Welsh family, and on the death of her husband returned with her baby son to settle in a cottage on the estate, near her old home. In later life he bought a house at Aberdyfi and when he was given a barony chose the title of Lord Aitkin of Aberdovey. He made important contributions in many fields of English law and helped to draw up the constitution of the Church in Wales.

Pennal, on the A.493 to Machynlleth, has a church

rebuilt early in the 19th century with memorials to the Thurston family of Talgarth Hall, west of the village. It is now a country hotel and car park. Pennal is believed to have been the site of the Roman fort of Maglona on the Roman road from Maridunum (Carmarthen) to Tomen-y-Mur, north of Trawsfynydd. Parts of the road can be traced still but the fort has disappeared, although Roman coins, pottery and other relics of Roman occupation have been found in the park of Talgarth Hall.

ABERGYNOLWYN is a small quarrymen's village with a station on the Tal-y-llyn Narrow Gauge Railway. It is set where the Cwm Dysynni, Cwm Fathew and Nant Gwernol meet, and towering above it are two peaks, over 2,000ft. high, of the 12-mile afforested range of the Tarens, which reaches from Tywyn to Corris. The small village museum has over 200 exhibits illustrating the way of life of the mining community, including old pictures of the Bryneglwys Quarries. The now disused quarries can be reached by a walk through a ravine. A so-called Roman Bridge crosses a little stream on the open mountainside. It was probably a packhorse bridge. The village of Tal-y-llyn and its lake are three miles to the north-east of Abergynolwyn.

ARTHOG, a mile east of Barmouth railway bridge, is delightfully set on the southern shore of the Mawddach estuary, against a background of the wooded lower slopes and craggy peaks of the Cadair Idris group. It was the opening of Barmouth Junction in 1865, and of the bridge two years later, which led to the purchase of land by a private company for the development of a small resort, with attractive terraced houses.

Arthog Falls, in the grounds of the castellated Arthog Hall, are half a mile from the now disused Arthog station. A short, steep path opposite the church passes the grounds of Tyn-y-Coed, a large house built in 1878, and continues upward to Llynnau Cregennen, two beautiful little tarns 800ft. above sea level, with the Tyrau-mawr, the 2,167ft. westerly summit of the Cadair range, towering above. The National Trust owns 700 acres of the area including the two lakes.

Bala, at the north-eastern end of Bala Lake (Llyn Tegid) has a long and unusually wide, tree-lined street. It has many interesting Welsh and English associations and a wealth of Arthurian and other legends. The Tomen-y-Bala, a mound behind the now disused Grammar School, is believed to be the site of Bala Castle, which was captured by Llywelyn the Great in 1202.

Bala was for centuries the chief market for goods knitted by both men and women in the cottages of the surrounding countryside. They specialized in gloves, stockings and woollen caps, known as 'Welsh wigs'. George III always wore Bala stockings during his bouts of rheumatism, and readers of Dickens's *Christmas Carol* will remember the jolly Mr. Fezziwig wore a Welsh wig. This cottage industry died out after the Industrial Revolution, but the Seren Centre established in 1971 displays examples of weaving, pottery and jewellery by modern craftsmen and has candlemaking workshops in an old Bala printing works. Two traditional hand looms are at work in the weaving studio producing traditional and original designs in rugs, shawls, cushion covers and scarves.

Bala became a busy centre of the Calvinistic Methodist movement after Thomas Charles married a Bala girl and settled there in 1783. He was then a curate in the Established Church but a year later became a member of the Methodist Society. He played a leading part in promoting Nonconformist Circulating Schools and Sunday Schools and in the foundation of the British and Foreign Bible Society after the well-known occasion when the need for Welsh Bibles was brought home to him by Mary Jones, who walked over the mountains from her home in Llanfihangel-y-Pennant, 25 miles away, to ask him for a Welsh Bible.

The house in which Thomas Charles lived was on the site now occupied by Barclays Bank. There is a statue of him outside Tegid Chapel and his grave is in the churchyard of Llanycil, a mile away beside the lake.

Charles's grandson, David Charles, who was born in Bala, was associated with his brother-in-law, Dr. Lewis Edwards, in founding a Calvinistic Methodist College of which Dr. Edwards was Principal for 50 years. It is now a Welsh Presbyterian Youth Centre. His statue is in front of the College and he, too, is buried in Llanycil churchyard.

The bronze statue in the main street commemorates Thomas Edward Ellis, Liberal M.P. for Meirionydd, who was born in 1859 at Cynlas farmhouse, about three miles north-east of Bala. He was a tireless worker in political, educational and religious affairs and was Chief Liberal Whip from 1894 until his death in 1899. His son, the late T.I. Ellis, who also played a leading part in Welsh life, was a member of the Welsh team in the early days of B.B.C.'s *Round Britain Quiz*.

Borrow wrote in praise of Bala, and Tennyson, who had a great love for the district, wrote part of *The Idylls of the King* whilst staying in the town.

Bala Grammar School, founded in 1712, numbered among its scholars such well-known Welshmen as Daniel Owen, the novelist, Tom Ellis, M.P., Sir Owen M. Edwards, historian and educationist, and Dr. John Puleston Jones, the blind preacher, who is commemorated by a plaque on a bakery in the High Street.

Lake Bala (Llyn Tegid) is 4½ miles long and a mile wide, and is completely encircled by lake-side roads. It was the largest sheet of privately owned water in the United Kingdom until the Glanllyn Estate, which includes the lake, was transferred to the Treasury in lieu of death duties on the estate of Sir William Watkins-Wynn of Wynnstay in 1944.

The lake is said to be the only place where the gwyniaid or Alpine fish, a species of *salmonid, genus Giregonus,* is found. This should not be confused with migratory trout, which are also known as gwyniaid. Pennant says they were taken from Llyn Tegid in great numbers in spring or summer. They do not rise or take any bait and can be caught only in nets. The average weight is half a pound, but they have been taken up to two pounds.

The simple little church of Llanycil is on the north-east of Llyn Tegid, between the A.494 and the water's edge. It has been much restored but has 18th and 19th century memorials to the Lloyd and Lloyd-Anwil families and to the Rev. Evan Lloyd, who was born at Fronfderw, Bala, and was a friend of David Garrick and John Wilkes. The latter composed the epitaph. The Rev. David Charles and other great Nonconformists are buried there.

The old Great Western Railway line from Ruabon to Barmouth, which skirted the southern shore of Bala Lake, was closed in 1965, but in 1971 the Rheilffordd Llyn Tegid Cyf. (Bala Lake Railway, Ltd.) was formed. It was the first railway preservation society registered in the Welsh language, and its 1ft. 11½ins. gauge track was the first narrow gauge railway ever laid on a standard gauge British Rail track. By 1972, a mile and a quarter of the railway had been opened and by 1976 the whole four and a half miles between Llanuwchllyn and Bala was in operation.

The Company has three historic little steam engines, one of which was the last steam locomotive to work in a slate quarry in Britain, and two fine diesel engines. A supporting Company, Cymdeithas Rheilfordd Llyn Tegid (Bala Lake Railway Society) assists in the day-to-day operations.

South-east of Bala and the Afon Dyfyrdwy (River Dee), which issues from Llyn Tegid to flow through the Vale of Llangollen to the sea at Chester, is Plas Rhiwaedog, a fine Jacobean mansion, now a Youth Hostel, where a branch of the Lloyd family lived from the

14th century to the beginning of the 19th century. The present house marks the traditional site of the home of Llywarch Hen, a 6th century warrior-prince. Both Sir John Morris-Jones and Sir Ifor Williams believed that the patriotic poems bearing his name were actually written by 9th century bards.

Llangower, on the B.4403 skirting the south-eastern side of Llyn Tegid, has a primitive little church restored in 1871. It has an elor-feirch (double horse bier). There is a similar bier at Llangelynin.

In the rebuilt church at Llanfor, a mile east of Bala on the A.494, are the colours of the Meirionethshire Milita, deposited there in 1914, and 18th century tablets to the Bulkeley family; also a hatchment and memorials to the Prices of Rhiwlas, whose mausoleum is in the churchyard with a doggerel verse over the entrance commemorating the fact that it was built with prize money won when Bendigo won the Kempton Park Jubilee in 1887.

Plas Rhiwlas, a mile north of Bala, was the seat of the Price family for over two centuries. They were descended from Rhys ap Meredydd (Rhys Fawr) of Foelas, who fought at the Battle of Bosworth. Richard John Lloyd Price, born in 1843, established the Welsh Whisky Distillery at Fron Goch and the Rhiwlas Brush Works. The distillery was demolished after the 1914-18 war and Plas Rhiwlas in 1955. A smaller house, designed by Sir Clough Williams-Ellis, was built on the site.

Bodiwan, nearby, was formerly the Independent College which was founded in Llanuwchllyn in 1841 but transferred to Bala the following year. After much bitter controversy it was amalgamated in 1892 as the Bala Bangor College at Bangor.

The A.4212 continues north-west from Rhiwlas beside the Afon Treweryn and the course of the abandoned branch line which once ran from Bala Junction to Blaenau Ffestiniog, skirting the northern shore of Llyn Celyn, the great reservoir of the Liverpool Corporation. It was created by flooding the upper Treweryn Valley and

Snowdon: view from the Summit

(Above) The stronghold of Castell-y-Bere, Meirionydd,
built by Llywelyn the Great in the shadow of Cadair Idris

Photo: Wales Tourist Board

(Below) Harlech, Castle, Meirionydd

drowning the village, from which the Welsh community was dispersed to seek new homes. The Liverpool Corporation built a chapel beside the lake, with slate memorials recording the names of those buried in the graveyard of Capel Celyn.

The Arenig Fawr and Arenig Fach rise on either side of the road, at the head of Llyn Celyn, each with its own small lake. On the summit of Arenig Fawr, over 2,000ft. above sea level, is a memorial to the crew of an American Flying Fortress which crashed on the peak in August 1943. A slate tablet gives the names and home States of the eight men who lost their lives. They were from Idaho, Illinois, Kentucky, New York, Ohio, California, Michigan and Pennsylvania.

In the years before the 1914-18 war Augustus John and his friend, I.D.Innes, stayed at Rhyd-y-Fen Inn (on the A.4212) and later rented a cottage beside the Nant-ddu brook for several seasons while they painted the Arenigs and Lake Bala.

B ARMOUTH (ABER MAWDDACH, or ABERMAW, or BERMO) is the largest of the family resorts of Meirionydd, although small compared with the great holiday towns on the North Wales coast. The greater part of the town is on level ground beside the sandy beach and long esplanade, but other houses and cottages climb the hills in a maze of winding lanes and steps which enable each to have an unobstructed view of the sea or the incomparable Mawddach Estuary. Wordsworth thought the estuary 'sublime', and no-one has yet been known to disagree. It has been painted by Richard Wilson, J.M.W.Turner and many other well-known artists. Darwin, who loved Barmouth, revised *The Origin of Species* and wrote part of *The Descent of Man* during a seven-week stay in a cottage beside the estuary.

Rock Terrace was given by a local resident to form part of Ruskin's first social experiment, the Guild of St.George, and the cottages are still administered by the

Ruskin Trust. Ruskin gives a description of his visit there in 1876 in *Fors Clavigera.*

The neighbouring hill of Dinas Oleu was given to the National Trust in 1875. It was the first property acquired by the Trust.

Barmouth was a busy port in the Middle Ages and Tŷ Gwyn yn Bermo, on the Quay, although modernized into cottages, has an ancient doorway dating back to the days when, it is said, the Vaughans of Corsygedol built it for the possible use of the young Earl of Richmond on his return from exile to gain the English throne as Henry VII.

Another curious relic is the early 19th century Round House, a small stone building in sand-dunes north of the harbour. It was a lock-up for roistering sailors, miners from the Bontddu mines and other law-breakers.

The parish church is at Llanaber, two miles away, but now part of Barmouth. The church was begun in 1200, took 50 years to complete and remains unaltered. It has been described as 'one of the greatest triumphs, for its size, of architectural genius and judgment'. It has a fine roof, an ancient chest carved out of a single log of wood, 18th century collecting boxes, and two 5th century inscribed stones. The unusual east window has a single lancet.

Barmouth is still served by British Rail (W.R.) and there is also a halt at Llanaber, but the most scenic railway approach, from Ruabon, is now only an enchanting memory. Although it was beautiful at all times of the year, I remember especially a journey in the winter of 1956 after a heavy fall of snow had transformed trees and rocks to a dazzlingly white fairyland. It was on that occasion I had the very great pleasure of spending an evening in the home of David Roberts (Telynor Mawddwy), the blind harpist of Barmouth, the centenary of whose birth was celebrated in 1975.

A Royal National Lifeboat Maritime Museum on Barmouth Quay has models of life-boats, yachts and other vessels, old and new equipment, medals and other fascinating exhibits.

Barmouth Bridge, across the mouth of the estuary, also has a footbridge giving access to the southern shore and a wonderful view up the estuary running far inland between the ranges of mountains either side.

Bontddu is an attractive village on the A.496 to Dolgellau, looking across the estuary to Cadair Idris. Gold was formerly mined in the Clogau mines, a mile inland from Bontddu. The mines have furnished sufficient gold for the wedding rings of the royal family, including H.M. Queen Elizabeth II.

Brithdir, on the B.4416, two and a half miles east of Dolgellau, is a scattered village on a section of an old Roman Road. It has a church built in 1896 by the widow of Charles Tooth in his memory. He was chaplain of the Anglican church of St.Mark's in Florence, of which St.Mark's, Brithdir, is a copy. The interior is a riot of Art Nouveau beaten copper fittings made by the Central School of Design in London.

A mile of the beautiful Torrent Walk is in the grounds of Plas Caerynwch which is reached from the A.487. Three-quarters of a mile away is Plas Caerynwch, near the junction of the B.4416 and the A.420. Caerynwch was originally a seat of the Vaughans, passed by marriage to the Humphreys in 1698 and again when the Humphreys heiress married Sir Richard Richards of Coed, who was Chief Baron of the Exchequer from 1817 until his death in 1823. A delightful manor-house is unaltered on the outside but the interior was restored in 1921 by Sir Clough Williams-Ellis. It stands in the grounds of the house built by Sir Richard Richards in 1786.

Brynmawr Farm near the Cross Foxes Inn, on the foothills of Cadair Idris, was the home of Rowland Ellis, the Quaker, who emigrated to Pennsylvania in 1686 with 100 of his neighbours. Brynmawr, the famous University for Women, stands on part of the estate near Philadelphia bought by Rowland Ellis which he called

Brynmawr after his Welsh home. The Halls of the University are called Meirion, Radnor, Denbigh and Pembroke. *Annerch i'r Cymru,* by Ellis Pugh, was the first Welsh book published in America. It was translated into English by Rowland Ellis. Pugh also emigrated in 1686 from the Dolgellau area.

CORRIS, four miles south-east of Tal-y-llyn, formerly a slate miners' village, is in two parts: one at the junction of Afon Dulas and a tributary stream, and Upper Corris on a steep slope which makes a perfect setting for Brynhyfryd, a mountain-side garden of specie rhododendrons and rare alpines.

Upper Corris lies below the main A.487 road and passers-by can look down over the roof tops and across the river to Aberllefenni, two miles away.

The Corris Railway, which had a gauge of 2ft. 3ins. and ran between Corris and Machynlleth, was opened as a tramway worked by horses in 1859, was named the Corris Railway in 1864, and changed to steam in 1879. The passenger services were suspended in 1931, a year after it was taken over by the Great Western Railway, and the line was closed in 1948 after nationalization.

The Corris Railway Society was formed in 1967 and a collection of equipment, pictures, timetables and other relics of the Corris Railway is now housed in buildings which were formerly part of the old Corris Station, beside the River Dulas, and two small lengths of track have been laid for the exhibition of rolling stock.

To-day there is little quarrying, and the local people are engaged chiefly in forestry work. The Llwyngwern Quarry, in Powys, just over the county border, which was one of the quarries served by the Corris Railway, is now a National Centre for Alternative Technology.

DINAS MAWDDWY is a very small village in spectacular scenery on the south-eastern border of the Snowdonia National Park. It is set in a deep, narrow valley on the A.470 from Dolgellau to Mallwyd and Machynlleth, with a steep descent from the Bwlch Oerddrws, 1,065ft. above sea level. The National Trust owns two mountain farms at the foot of Bwlch Oerddrws, just north of the A.458, which are good examples of early Welsh farm-house architecture.

Dinas Mawddwy is the best centre for climbing the Aran range, of which the highest, Aran Fawddwy, is 2,970ft. - the highest peak in Wales south of the Snowdon range - cradles the little Craiglyn Dyfi in a deep hollow. Its northern neighbour, Aran Benllyn, is 70ft. lower but has an equally daunting aspect on the steep, craggy south side, particularly from Cwm Cywarch.

The mountains around Dinas Mawddwy are as distinct in character from those of the Snowdon group, or those south of the Dyfi estuary, as the men of the district have been from the earliest times in their physical characteristics. Even today, the majority have a reddish tinge to their hair.

It is said that Prince Maelgwn granted St. Tydecho the right of sanctuary for the district, with the usual result that in the course of time it became a haunt of robbers. The Gwylliad Cochion Mawddwy (the Red Bandits of Mawddwy) were so notorious for the terror they inspired that their fame has lived on to the present day. Eventually Sir John Wynn of Gwydir and Baron Lewis Owen, Vice Chamberlain of North Wales, succeeded in capturing more than 80 of the band, and they were put to death in 1554. A year later, Owen was ambushed by the remnant of the bandits at Llediart-y-Baron (Baron's Gate) in Cwm Clywedog and he and his son-in-law were killed, but official retribution followed and the gang was finally extirpated.

The villagers of Dinas Mawddwy formed a close-knit community and the unemployment which followed the closure of the quarries entailed much hardship which was partly alleviated by the opening in 1949 of the Meirion Mill, which is housed in an old quarry building. The exclusive Meirion tapestry quilts are woven there and traditional and modern Welsh woollen and flannel goods are made, including blankets, tweeds, clothes, furnishing fabrics and gift items, which are sold in the shop. Light meals are obtainable and there is a special children's playground.

Dinas Mawddwy once belonged to the Princes of Powys but eventually passed by marriage to the Mytton family, from whom the notorious 18th century Shropshire squire and 'sportsman', Jack Mytton, was descended. His wild extravagance and eccentricity, amounting at times to the verge of madness, included such minor pranks as offering the children of Dinas sums ranging from half-crowns to half-guineas for the senseless exploit of rolling down Moel Dinas. Despite his eccentricity he was High Sheriff of Meirionydd in 1821, but his extravagance resulted in his death in a debtors' prison in 1834.

Llanymawddwy, 4½ miles north-east of Dinas Mawddwy, is reached by the road through Cwm Cywarch, where magpies, buzzards, jays and hares abound. There is a cluster of houses and a simple little church dedicated to St.Tydecho, which has an early medieval font, a Jacobean communion table in the vestry and low clipped yew trees lining the path to the doorway.

The road continues north to Llanuwchllyn over Bwlch y Groes through even grander scenery than that of the Bwlch Oerddrws. It is more suitable for walkers than motorists of a nervous disposition, or cyclists, for it rises from 634ft. to 1,790ft. in little over a mile; the last 200 yards to the summit being 1 in 4½. Bwlch y Groes is the highest pass in North Wales and has been used for Motor Association rally trials. A steep and narrow road drops down from the summit on the east to Lake Vyrnwy in Powys.

DOLGELLAU is nine miles east of Barmouth, where the A.494 and the A.470 are linked by a 17th century bridge across the Afon Wnion. It is an essentially Welsh town which seems to have grown naturally out of its splendid setting of mountains. The queer angles at which so many of the sturdy stone houses have been built create narrow, crooked streets which are a town-planners' nightmare and the joy of artists and photographers. Strangely enough, in spite of its predominently Welsh-speaking population, many of the street names have a familiar ring to English ears - Baker Street, Finsbury Square, Smithfield Street, Lombard Street, and several others.

Although the greater part of the town dates from the early 19th century, Dolgellau has a long history and a few older buildings remain, but the house traditionally associated with the Parliament held by Owain Glyndŵr in May, 1404, was bodily removed to Newtown, Montgomeryshire, in 1882. It was from this Parliament that he dispatched two envoys with a letter to Charles VI, which resulted in a treaty of alliance between Wales and France.

The Grammar School for boys, founded in the 17th century, has removed from the old building at the foot of the road to Cadair Idris to a more modern building on the Machynlleth road.

Dr. Williams's Boarding School for Girls, on the Barmouth road, still one of the best-known in Wales, was founded in 1875.

The town cricket team claims to be the oldest in Wales. It was founded in 1841 by Frederick Temple, then a Balliol undergraduate and later Archbishop of Canterbury.

The parish church was rebuilt in the 18th century on an earlier site and has a simple medieval west tower. The high boarded roof of the interior is supported on four long oak poles on either side, between the nave and the aisles. The poles were drawn by oxen from Dinas Mawddwy over the steep pass of Bwlch Oerddrws. The church also has the bowl of an alabaster font, dated 1651 and an exceptionally well-preserved 14th century effigy of a knight with a lion carved on the shield, representing Meurig, son of Ynyr Fychan, an ancestor of the Nanneys and Vaughans. Also a monument to Lord Chief Baron Richard Richards, who was born in Dolgellau in 1752. In the churchyard is a conspicuous pyramidal monument to David Richards (Dafydd Ionawr) a schoolmaster and poet, who taught at Dolgellau Grammar School from 1800 to 1807.

Y Marian, the meadow beside the Afon Wnion, is the playground of Dolgellau. Few places have finer common land, with the crags of Cadair Idris towering above it on the south and the river skirting it on the north.

The Cadair Idris range, second only to Snowdon in popularity among Welsh mountains, runs parallel with the southern shore of the Mawddach estuary and is at its steepest overlooking Dolgellau. Legends connect the so-called 'Chair of Idris' with a giant of that name, or with King Arthur, and it was said that anyone who slept there was found in the morning as a corpse, a madman or a bard. Elves and fairies of friendly disposition are said to inhabit its caves.

It is a long ridge, chiefly of old volcanic rocks, extending from Arthog to Cross Foxes and at its highest in the centre where Pen-y-Gadair reaches 2,927ft., about four miles from Dolgellau. Each of the deep cwms on either side of the distinctive and easily recognizable peak cradles a lake surrounded by precipitous cliffs. There are at least eight routes up Cadair, three of which are from Dolgellau.

Owen Glynne Jones, who made a rock climb on the face of Cadair Idris in 1888, was one of the founders of British rock climbing. Some years later Arnold Lunn injured his leg so badly at Cross Foxes that he turned his attention to ski-ing, a sport which he afterwards revolutionized.

In the 18th century nearly every poor man in the town, and every farmer in the neighbourhood, had his loom on which he and his family made webs, a coarse woollen cloth of flannel for which Dolgellau was so famous that it was said the trade was valued at £100,000 annually. The only hint of this cottage industry today is in the number of ruined pandau on the banks of the mountain streams.

High and low life in Dolgellau, Plas Hengwrt, and the neighbourhood, are vividly recalled in the manuscript diary of Elizabeth Baker, now in the National Library of Wales. *The Old Order,* a slim paper-back by Sir Ben Bowen Thomas, published in 1948, is based on extracts from the Diary. It reflects the life of a countryside, still almost entirely agricultural, in which the social and economic life revolved around the market towns. Elizabeth Baker died at Dolgellau in 1789, at the age of 69.

Dolgellau was a great coaching centre in the 18th century and there were a number of good coaching inns, some of which survive. The Golden Lion Royal Hotel, originally known as Plas Isa, had stabling for 100 horses. Twenty Welsh ponies carried visitors to the summit of Cadair Idris including, it is said, 'many of the crowned heads of Europe'.

The innumerable walks and drives in the neighbourhood include the Torrent Walk and the two Precipice Walks, with entrancing views of Cwm Wnion and the glorious estuary of the Mawddach.

Penmaenpool, two miles west of Dolgellau, at the head of the Mawddach estuary, has a toll bridge across the Afon Wnion which also links the A.496 and the A.493. Like many of the hamlets of the Cwm Wnion, it once had its own railway station but now the nearest is at Barmouth Junction. It can still be reached by boat up the Mawddach estuary as well as by the roads along the north and south banks of the Mawddach.

FAIRBOURNE (Y FRIOG), two miles south of the Mawddach estuary, is on level ground between a magnificent sandy beach and the foothills of Cadair Idris. The superb site was bought by a private company, headed by Mr. McDougall of Self-Raising Flour fame, in the

19th century and developed as a rival to the newly built family resort of Arthog.

Although the Coastal Section of the old Cambrian Railway (now British Rail, W.R.) reached Barmouth Junction in 1865 and the bridge over the estuary was opened two years later, it was not until 1912 that a station was provided at Fairbourne, and the parish church was not built until 1926.

One of the greatest joys of Fairbourne is its Miniature Railway. The horse-drawn tramway which conveyed building material to Fairbourne began providing passenger cars for visitors in 1890. It was then 1⅛ of a mile long and had a 2 ft. gauge, which was converted in 1916 to a 15 ins. gauge with steam traction. Small as it is, it can carry adults as well as children. It is now two miles long with one terminus close to the main line station and the A.493 main road from Tywyn to Dolgellau, and the other terminus at Penrhyn Point, connecting with the Ferry Service to Barmouth, on the north side of the estuary. The line runs so close to the seashore that in abnormally stormy weather the service has to be cancelled, and a flag is flown at Barmouth Ferry to indicate when the trains are running.

The Miniature Railway suffered badly from neglect during the World War of 1939-45 and all the original rolling stock disappeared. The line was bought by three West Midland industrialists in 1946, repaired, and supplied with new engines and with closed and open coaches. In 1951 a newly designed Mobile Canteen was provided, equipped with gas heating facilities and an electric refrigerator, providing light refreshments. It is believed to have been the first of its kind in Britain.

FFESTINIOG or LLAN FFESTINIOG, on the A.470, which runs south to Dolgellau past Trawsfynydd Lake, is a small market town in the wide pastoral Vale of Ffestiniog, bounded by wooded hills and craggy mountains. The Cynfal Falls, in a richly wooded cwm, are half a mile to the south of Ffestiniog. A high, peculiarly shaped rock rising from the middle of the Afon Cynfal is known as Huw Llwyd's Pulpit. Llwyd was a 'bard, magician and warrior' who is said to have stood on the rock to chant his midnight incantations. He died about 1620. Ffestiniog is described under the name of 'Llan dhu', and the falls as 'Cwm dhu', in Mrs. Gaskell's novel *Ruth*. There is a splendid view down the Vale of Ffestiniog from the churchyard.

The early 17th century exterior of Cynfal Fawr, south of Rhaeadr Cynfal, hides an earlier interior with huge cruck beams, which is believed to have been built by Huw Llwyd. The interior and exterior of the earlier house are described in a cywydd (lyric poem) by Huw Machno c. 1630. Huw Llwyd was not only reputed to be a warrior, bard and magician but a famous sportsman, and some of his best poems relate to foxes and hounds. He fought in France and the Netherlands in a Welsh regiment and it is said he was away so long that on his return he was not recognised by his family. The incident is recorded in verse in Peacock's *Headlong Hall*.

Cynfal Fawr is now a riding school, but a plaque beside the house commemorates Huw's grandson, Morgan Llwyd, who served in the Parliamentarian army but signed *A Word for God* when Cromwell appointed himself Lord Protector. Morgan Llwyd wrote *Llyfr y Tri Aderyn* (The Book of the Three Birds), a dialogue between The Eagle (Cromwell), the Dove (a Puritan) and the Raven (an Episcopalian), one of the classics of the Welsh language.

Plas Dol-y-moch, near Dduault station, was built in 1643. It has a gabled end, dormer windows, a stone staircase and coats of arms in plaster-work.

Blaenau Ffestiniog is a quarryman's town, magnificently set in a horseshoe of mountains at the head of the Vale of Ffestiniog, 750 ft. above sea level. It is the southern terminus of a branch railway line from Llandudno Junction which has survived the Beeching

Axe, but the old line from Bala has closed and the Ffestiniog Narrow Gauge Railway from Porthmadog now stops short at Llyn Ystradau, two miles beyond Ddualt.

Blaenau Ffestiniog is the largest town in Meirionydd and a place of great individuality, built of bluish slate which has been used for street-paving, roofing and fencing. It is overhung by the precipitous crags of the Moelwyn and Manod ranges which rise to over 2,500 ft. Among the many small lakes in the neighbourhood is Llyn Barlwyd which, in common with some other Welsh lakes, has a treacherous 'floating island' of peat which sinks if stepped upon. Llyn Stwlan has been enlarged to form an upper reservoir for the Tan-y-Grisiau Reservoir, 1,000 ft. below, with a Hydro-Electric Power Station on its west bank.

The Manod range has quarries extending far under the mountains in which paintings from London's National Gallery were stored for safety during the 1939-45 war. The Gloddfa Ganol museum at the Ffestiniog Mountain Tourist Centre, on the A.470 north of Blaenau, displays massive machinery from the slate era, relates the history of slate and its people and their struggles and arranges Landrover tours to the mountain top. Visitors are equipped with miners' helmets and lights for the guided tour into Nyth y Gigfran Quarry.

The Llechwedd slate mine, also on the A.470, has specially designed passenger cars drawn by battery-driven locomotives which carry visitors through the network of tunnels where Victorian mining conditions have been re-created with genuine period equipment and tableaux. Old machinery is also displayed in a slate mill. Visitors are advised to wear warm clothing, as the underground temperature remains constant at 50 deg. Fahrenheit (10 deg. Centigrade). The Llechwedd Slate Caverns were first opened to the public in 1972 and within nine months won both the British Touring Authority's 'Come to Britain' trophy and the Festival of

Wales Trophy of the Wales Tourist Board. A variety of goods can be bought in the slate-crafts workshop, where also house name-plates can be carved while the customer waits.

Although use was made of the surface slates for roofing from the earliest times in the neighbourhood of Blaenau, it was not until the late 18th century that any attempt was made to exploit them. Then, instead of a single wealthy landowner, as in other North Wales slate quarries, Blaenau was worked by a little company of quarrymen, and many tales are told of their prodigious feats. They even walked to ports as distant as Bristol or London to dispose of cargoes of slates sent by sea. As the owner of the property lived far away and took no interest in it, they were not hampered by having to pay ground rent, but at the beginning of the 19th century the property was sold and the quarrymen were too late to bid for it. The Lancashire men who made the successful bid had hardly more capital than the quarrymen but were successful in persuading rich businessmen to back them. They built up the venture with the same frugality and energy as the quarrymen had done, walking to and from Bangor and Holyhead with the proceeds of sales, to enable them to carry out developments. In the earliest days pack mules were used to carry the slates to the coast for shipment, and it was not until the first load of slates was conveyed to the new port of Porthmadog by the Ffestiniog Railway in 1836 that the great days of Blaenau Ffestiniog really began. Blaenau slates are still shipped to the most distant parts of the world, but now there are only a few hundreds of men where at the peak period over 3,000 were employed.

GANLLWYD, a small village on the A.470, is in the Coed y Brenin (King's Forest), which covers an area of 15,600 acres north of Dolgellau. A great part of the Forest was bought from the Vaughans of Nannau in the early 1920's and was originally called Vaughan Forest.

The name was changed in 1935 to commemorate the Silver Jubilee of George V.

The Forest is completely surrounded by mountains - Cadair Idris, Rhobell Fawr, Aran Fawddwy and the Rhinogs - and there are many rivers and waterfalls in the lovely mixed woodlands of beech, oak, wild cherry, lime, larch, spruce and fir. Fallow deer roam the Forest and there are three Forest Trails. The Maesgwm Visitor Centre is among the first of its kind in Wales.

The National Trust owns over 1,000 acres of the Forest, including two hotels - Tyn-y-groes and Dolmelynllyn. The attractive gabled Tyn-y-groes hotel was originally a coaching inn. On the other side of the road there is a precipitous drop to the wooded valley of the Afon Mawddach. Dolmelynllyn is on a slope above the A.470, just before the village of Ganllwyd is reached.

Nannau, 800 ft. above Dolgellau, on the slope of Foel Offrwn and close to Llyn Cynwch, was the seat of the Nanney, or Nannau, family who were descended from Ynyr Hen, who flourished in 1200-50 and whose grandson, Meurig Fychan, is buried in Dolgellau church. Nannau is associated with legends of a feud between Owain Glyndŵr and Hywel Sele and of a haunted oak, referred to in Scott's *Marmion*, but for which there appears to be no historical foundation.

Contemporary bards say Nannau was rebuilt by Huw Nannau Hen (who died in 1623) on a grand scale. His grand-daughter married the antiquary, Robert Vaughan of Hengwrt, and their grandson, also Robert Vaughan, married the heiress of Col. Hugh Nanney in 1719. Nannau is now a three-storied Georgian house. There are memorials to the Vaughans in Llanfachreth church, north-east of Nannau.

In 1948 Rhyd-y-main, another of the Forest villages, just off the A.494 in Cwm Wnion, was chosen amid much local excitement as the setting for the film *The Last Days of Dolwen*, of which Emlyn Williams was author, co-director and star.

HARLECH. The castle and ancient village of Harlech are on a crag 200 ft. above the great expanse of Morfa Harlech, which was once covered by the sea but is now the site of the railway station and the golf course and is traversed by the A.496

The castle was built by Edward I between 1285 and 1290 at a cost of just over £8,000. It is a massive square building measuring 70 yds. along each side, with four 20 ft. high round bastions at each angle and one on either side of the entrance, and a lofty inner ward, curtain-walls and towers 40 ft. high. It contains a great hall for the garrison, a chapel, kitchens, a bakehouse and many spacious rooms in its upper storeys.

During the Glyndŵr rising it was defended for the king from 1400 to 1404 and surrendered only after Glyndŵr himself took charge of the siege, and then only when sickness and starvation had reduced the garrison to 21 men.

Glyndŵr made Harlech his Court and chief arsenal. He brought his personal treasure there as well as his wife, one of his daughters, who had married Edmund Mortimer, and his grandchildren, and appointed Mortimer the castellan. Glyndŵr held his second Parliament at Harlech in August, 1405. During the eight months when Mortimer was besieged there, Glyndŵr made desperate attempts to rescue his family and the garrison but it proved impossible to break the blockade. Mortimer died of exhaustion and semi-starvation in January, 1409, and the garrison was forced to surrender. Glyndŵr's family and possessions were seized and taken to London, where Mortimer's wife, little son, and two of his three infant daughters died within three weeks in consequence of their privations during the siege.

During the Wars of the Roses the Lancastrian Jasper Tudor, Earl of Pembroke, half-brother of Henry VI, made Harlech his headquarters after the Battle of Towton in 1461 and appointed Dafydd ap Jevan ab Einion castellan. Sir Dafydd held out long after Jasper had fled to Brittany, and did not surrender until 1468 when starvation forced him to yield to William, Lord Herbert, and his brother, Sir Richard Herbert, on honourable terms. Lord Herbert was rewarded with the forfeited earldom of Pembroke. Sir Dafydd is said to have boasted that he had 'in his youth maintained a castle in France so long that every old woman in Wales had heard of it, and in his old age he had held a castle in Wales so long that every old woman in France had heard of it'.

It is thought that it was an incident in this siege which inspired the well-known march *Gŵr Harlech* (Men of Harlech).

In the Civil Wars of Charles I Harlech was so remote from the other centres of Parliamentary activity that it was not attacked until all the other castles had submitted. It was surrendered on honourable terms by Col. William Owen, the royalist governor, on 13 March, 1647, to Col. Jones, Cromwell's Welsh brother-in-law. Although some attempt was made to 'slight' it, the immense strength of the main buildings has kept them almost perfect, apart from the roofs, until the present day.

The 'Garden Tower' is also known as 'Mortimer's Tower', recalling his gallant defence, and the 'Weathercock Tower' is sometimes called 'Branwen's Tower', recalling one of the many legends and romances associated with the castle. Her tragic story is told in *The Mabinogion*. Branwen, the 'White-bosomed', sister of Bran the Blessed and daughter of Llyr (Shakespeare's King Lear), was courted at Harlech by Matholwch, King of Ireland, but suffered many humiliations and sorrows through the meddling of her spiteful step-brother.

Harlech's grandeur and stirring history is reflected in *Harlech*, an awdl (ode) by my late husband, Treffîn, with which he won the Chair competition at Wrexham Eisteddfod in 1933.

Edward I made Harlech an English borough and it was once the county town of Meirionydd, but it had comparatively little importance apart from the castle. It is now a village of tortuous narrow streets. Houses of various periods since the 18th century straggle picturesquely along the B.4575 behind the castle.

The church dates only from 1840 but has stained glass from the Celtic Studios of Swansea in the south window and a 15th century font from the older church of Llandanwg, on the seashore between Llanfair and Llandanwg station. St. Tanwg's was restored by the Society for the Preservation of Ancient Monuments. It has an early 15th century east window, the lintel of which is formed by a 5th or 6th century pillar stone with a beautifully incised inscription. There is also a 6th century fragment with an unusual form of inscription. St. Tanwg's is open only occasionally for services during the summer.

The National Trust owns about an acre of land between Harlech and Llanfair, with footpaths to the sea.

Coleg Harlech, founded in 1927 under the inspiration of Dr. Thomas Jones, C.H., who was Founder President until his death in 1955, is a residential adult education college providing yearly courses and summer schools in beautiful surroundings. Henry Gethin Lewis, who gave the original building, an imposing granite house dating from 1910, summed up the aims of the college: 'To enlarge the vision of its students, to develop their latent capabilities for leadership, and to stimulate their mental and spiritual growth'. There are no examinations or diplomas, but opportunities are offered for a liberal education to working men and women who have proved their enthusiasm and capacity for further education by their record of attendance at extra-mural classes. It is non-profit making, and a small number of scholarships are given by Trade Unions.

The majority of the students are Welsh, but there are also students from Europe, the U.S.A. and African States. The Coleg Harlech Arts Centre holds exhibitions of works by local, national and international artists, which are open free to the public.

There are many sites of antiquarian interest in the hills behind Harlech. Eight acres of Llechwedd Wood, just north of Harlech, were given by Mrs. Graves to the National Trust in memory of her husband, Alfred Perceval Graves (Canwr Cilarné), who was born in Dublin but spent the last years of his life in Harlech where he wrote his autobiography *To Return to All That*, a reply to his son Robert's *Good-bye to All That*. His original books of verse, songs and ballads are on Irish and Welsh subjects. The best-known is probably *Father O'Flynn and Other Lyrics*.

Another three acres were given to the Trust by the executors of Miss Lily Graves.

Farther north along the B.4573 on the side of a hillock called Glas Ynys (the Green Isle), is Y Lasynys, a small Elizabethan house which was the birthplace of the Rev. Ellis Wynne, author of the Welsh prose classic *Gweledigaetheu y Bardd Cwsc* (Visions of the Sleeping Bard). He became incumbent of Llanfair-juxta-Harlech in 1711 and is buried there. The little church has a well-preserved 15th century roof, an early 17th century oak chancel screen and memorial tablets to the Owen family of Crafnant tracing their descent back to the 16th century. Crafnant, now a farmhouse, is in the beautiful Cwm Artro.

LLANBEDR, on the Afon Artro, south of Harlech, is a large and attractive village of tree-shaded stone-built houses which many anglers have voted one of the best places in North Wales for trout and sewin. It is on the sandy reach of the Morfa Dyffryn which lies between the foothills of Ardudwy and the sea.

Llanbedr church, once a Chapel of Ease for Llandanwg, has a Bronze Age stone with spiral ornamentation, unique in Wales and rarely seen elsewhere. A slate slab brought from Llandanwg church has a Welsh verse reminding the reader that no one should enter the presence of God in this holy place unless he is of good mind. It is the work of Matthew Owen, born in the Vale of Edeyrnion in 1631, whose englyn can be seen above many church porches in Meirionydd and Denbighshire.

A spit of land known as Mochras, or Shell Island, close to Llanbedr and Pensarn station, abounds in shells, of which many different varieties have been found. It protects a lagoon-like natural harbour which is a favourite yachting centre. A drilling rig on the Mochras Peninsula was built by the Institute of Geological Sciences to explore the bed of Cardigan Bay as part of a seismic survey programme.

The early 17th century Mochras Farm has been modernized inside. During the summer months it has many visitors, who are apparently undeterred by the low-flying planes from the neighbouring airfield.

The 18th century Salem Baptist Chapel, a mile up Cwm Artro, was the setting for Sydney Curnow Vosper's famous painting, *Salem Chapel*, dominated by the striking figure of an old woman in Welsh costume, which was hung at the Royal Academy in 1909 and is now in the Lever Gallery, Port Sunlight. Thousands of reproductions have been made of it which hang in many Welsh homes in all parts of the world.

Llanbedr is the best starting point for Llyn Cwm Bychan, locally known as the Water-lily lake, a wild and lonely tarn of deep blue water, 505 ft. above sea-level. Craig-y-Saeth (Rock of the Arrow) on the south is well-known for its echo.

The so-called Roman Steps, a series of over 2,000 unhewn slabs of rock, of unknown origin but probably medieval, form a staircase running upward from the Llyn to the pass of Bwlch y Tyddiad, 1,294 ft. above sea level and 7½ miles from Llanbedr. At the top of the Roman Steps there is a path to Drws Ardudwy, the pass between Rhinog Fawr and Rhinog Fach, east of which is the Coed y Brenin Forest Park. Two miles from the entry to Drws Ardudwy is Maesygarnedd, birthplace of Colonel John

Jones, who married Cromwell's sister Catherine and was one of the judges who condemned Charles I. He was descended from Ynyr Fychan, Lord of Nannau, and whatever may be thought of his politics, he was a brave and successful soldier.

LLANDDERFEL, on the B.4402 east of Bala, is grouped round its church, which was restored in the 1870's but still has a fine screen, with massive lower timbers, rich carving above and a rood-loft over it. In the church porch are a wooden staff and the shattered relics of a curious wooden animal, variously described as a lion, a horse and a stag, which is all that remains of the wooden image of St. Derfel the Mighty which attracted hundreds of pilgrims in the Middle Ages. It was credited by many with the power to put out forest fires, although there are some accounts which say it was predicted that one day it would 'set a forest on fire'. The villagers were so reluctant to let Thomas Cromwell's Commissioners take away the image of their patron saint that they offered the then large sum of £40 for permission to keep it. The Commissioners refused, and it was used in 1528 for the burning of a friar named Forest, thus gruesomely fulfilling the old prophecy. The scene is described in The *Fifth Queen* by Ford Madox Brown.

A number of members of the Society of Friends emigrated to the New World from this district in the reign of Charles II, and gave local names to their settlements in the neighbourhood of Philadelphia.

Edward Jones (Bardd y Brenin), harpist, publisher and arranger of Welsh harp music, was born at Henblas, Llandderfel, in 1752. He was appointed harpist to the Prince of Wales about 1790 and on the prince's accession to the throne as George IV, was known as 'the King's Bard'.

LLANDDWYWE is on the A.496, south of Dyffryn Ardudwy station. The church stands in a circular churchyard. It dates from 1593 and has a chapel added in the early 17th century in which are effigies and memorials of the Vaughans of Corsygedol, including an elaborate 17th century group.

The 17th century entrance lodge to the long drive up to Corsygedol is opposite the church, but the house cannot be seen from the road. It is one of the finest houses in Meirionydd, dating back in part to the 16th century, and has beautiful panelled rooms. It was the seat of the Fychans, or Vaughans, for centuries.

An old account described Gruffydd Vaughan as 'in great credit with Jasper, Earl of Pembroke, who lay in his house at Corsygedol when he fled to France in the time of Edward IV, and as some report, Harry, the Earl of Richmond with him, who afterwards was King of England.' Gruffydd was subsequently 'squire of the Body' to Henry VII. A later Vaughan, who was M.P. for Meirionydd in the reign of Charles I, was so fat that the folding doors of the House of Commons always had to be opened for him.

Near Corsygedol are the remains of several prehistoric burial chambers, a stone circle, a large cromlech called Coetan Arthur, said to have been thrown by King Arthur from the top of Moelfre, a neighbouring hill 1,932ft. high, and still bearing the impress of his fingers, and the Corsygedol Lakes - Llyn Irddyn, 1,000 feet above sea level, Llyn Bodlyn (the Barmouth Waterworks), 1,245 ft., and the smaller Llyn Dulyn.

Half a mile south of Llanddwywe is the pretty village of Tal-y-bont, near the mouth of the Afon Ysgethin, which rises in Llyn Bodlyn, below the precipitous crag of Diffwys.

LLANEGRYN, on the Afon Dysynni, lies in a hollow just off the A.493 to Tywyn. An obelisk in Ebenezer chapel commemorates Hugh Owen (1639-1700), the Independent 'Apostle of Meirionydd', who inherited Bron-y-clwydwr in Llanegryn parish which he made his headquarters as overseer of the Independent Nonconformists of Meirionydd. He suffered considerable hardships before the passing of the Toleration Act. He has been described as 'a diligent preacher of great serenity of temperament'.

The parish church of Llanegryn is on high ground north-west of the village. It was restored in the late Victorian era but retains two 13th century windows and a wonderful 15th century screen and rood-loft with elaborate carving of exceptional delicacy. There is also a medieval font and handsome monuments to the Owens and Wynnes of nearby Plas Peniarth.

There is a long drive to the house, which was rebuilt about 1700 on a much earlier foundation and is neighboured by another building dating from 1727, surmounted by a bell-tower. The property came into the possession of the Wynnes in 1771, by marriage. The Wynnes of Peniarth have been one of the leading Welsh families and include William Watkin Edward Wynne, the indefatigable 19th century antiquary and genealogist who was one of the founders of the Cambrian Archaeological Association. He was also a good amateur architect and supervised the restoration of the churches of Llanegryn, Tywyn and Llanaber. He made Peniarth a centre of Welsh culture and was generous in making his priceless collection of old Welsh MSS. and books available to scholars. His library included books from Hengwrt, near Llanelltud, which were bequeathed to him in 1859. After the death of his sons, the bulk of the collection was bought by Sir John Williams who gave them to the newly-founded National Library of Wales.

LLANELLTUD is at the junction of the A.470, which runs north from Dolgellau through Coed y Brenin to Blaenau Ffestiniog, the A.494 from Bala and the A.496 to Barmouth.

The small and beautifully kept village has a church set on rising ground at its entrance. Although much restored, it has an old oak roof, an ancient font and a hatchment of a Vaughan of Hengwrt. Frances Power Cobbe, the 19th century philanthropist and religious writer, who spent the last 20 years of her life at Hengwrt, is buried in the circular churchyard. The two Precipice Walks, with their spectacular views, start near Llanelltud.

Cymer Abbey, just across the Mawddach from Llanelltud, can be seen clearly from the bridge on the A.494, at the tidal limit of the Mawddach estuary. The *Brut y Tywysogyon* (Chronicle of the Princes) records that the Abbey of Cwmhir in Radnorshire sent a colony of monks to Cymer at the end of the 12th century. Cymer was the second Cistercian monastery in Wales. It was endowed by the grandsons of the poet prince, Owain Gwynedd, but the ensuing wars with the English left the little community far from wealthy. When it was suppressed in 1536, the site was acquired by the Vaughans of Nannau. The roofless remains of the 13th century church and a 14th century tower remain, with the outlines of the cloister and frater, but the Chapter House, day room and reredorter have completely disappeared.

A chalice and paten found in the neighbouring hills by two gold prospectors, and believed to have belonged to the abbey, are now in the National Museum of Wales at Cardiff.

The plain but attractive Georgian mansion of Hengwrt stood on rising ground near Cymer Abbey until a few years ago, when it was destroyed by fire. The Hengwrt MSS. collected by Robert Vaughan, the 17th century historian and antiquary, who is regarded as one of the chief benefactors of Welsh scholarship, included *The Black Book of Carmarthen*, *The Book of Taliesin*, the earliest examples of Welsh poetry and prose, and the Hengwrt Chaucer, one of the seven manuscripts printed by the Chaucer Society. The manuscripts remained at Hengwrt until the death in 1859 of Sir Robert Williams Vaughan of Nannau, Hengwrt and Rug, who bequeathed them to his friend, W.W.E. Wynne of Peniarth. They are

143

now in the National Library of Wales.

LLANENDDWYN and its church, dedicated to St. Enddwyn, a female Celtic saint, are close to Dyffryn Ardudwy station, on the coast. The church was largely rebuilt in 1883. It has a 16th century roof and finial and a stone with an incised spiral in the gable of its lychgate. Col. John Jones of Maesygarnedd, the regicide, is buried there. On the south of the neighbouring village of Dyffryn Ardudwy, on the A.496, are two Neolithic dolmen at the back of the school. Just north, the peak of Snowdon comes into view. The Sarn Badrig, which stretches for about 10 miles out to sea, has been proved by modern research to be a natural formation but many legends of its origin still cling to it. It was long believed to be one of the embankments of the Cantref-y-Gwaelod, which was overwhelmed by the waves in very early times. It is not known why the name of St. Patrick is associated with the causeway.

LLANFIHANGEL-Y-PENNANT, two and a half miles from Abergwynolwyn, in the Cwm at the south-west of Cadair Idris watered by the Afon Cadair, is a small village clustering round a church dating from the 15th century. Its fame lies in the story of Mary Jones, who was born in a cottage on the slopes of Cadair Idris, just above the village. The cottage is now in ruins but a memorial was erected there in 1907 by the Sunday Schools of Meirionydd, telling of her journey in 1800 when she walked across the mountains to Bala, 25 miles away, to procure a copy of the Welsh Bible from the Rev. Thomas Charles. On arrival at Bala, she was told there were no more Bibles left for distribution, but when Charles saw her distress and realized how far she had walked, he gave her his own treasured copy. It was this incident which prompted him to play a leading part in the foundation of the British and Foreign Bible Society. Mary is buried at Bryn-crug, near Tywyn.

Llanegryn Church, Meirionydd

Photo: Wales Tourist Board

Tan-y-Bwlch, Meirionydd

There is a comparatively easy track from Llanfihangel-y-Pennant to the summit of Cadair Idris, the western face of which is not so precipitous as it is on the north and east.

South-west of the village, near the confluence of the Afon Cadair with the Dysynni, are the remains of Castell y Bere. *The Brut y Tywysogyon* (Chronicle of the Princes) records that in the year 1221 Llywelyn the Great deprived his son Gruffydd of the cantref (Hundred) of Meirionydd and began to build in it a castle for himself. It was afterwards occupied by Dafydd, brother of Llywelyn the Last, in his resistance to Edward I. He escaped to Snowdon after it surrendered, but eventually suffered a barbarous execution at Shrewsbury.

Excavations have shown that Castell-y-Bere has far more architectural embellishments than the other castles of purely Welsh origin. Some of the sculptured capitals are now in the National Museum of Wales at Cardiff. The remains are now rather scanty, but the outlines of the castle can be traced and the beauty and peace of its surroundings make it well worth a visit.

On the road down Cwm Dysynni to Llanegryn and Tywyn is Caer Berllan, a small gem of a 17th century manor-house, and Craig-yr-Aderyn (Bird Rock), where the sea once reached and sea-birds still nest.

LLANUWCHLLYN, a mile south-west of Llyn Tegid (Bala Lake), is strung out for nearly a mile along the B.4403, with a bridge over the Afon Twrch at one end and another across the Afon Dyfrdwy at the other.

The church is late Victorian, on the site of a much older building, and has a well-preserved recumbent effigy of Ieuan ap Gruffydd of Glanllyn in plate armour over a mailed coat, dated 1370. There is also a portable 19th century wooden baptistry.

The former Great Western Railway station is now the Headquarters of the Bala Lake Railway. The village school (now a cottage) was built in 1841 to celebrate the coming of age of Sir Watkin Williams Wynn, 6th baronet, and the village pump commemorates the birth of his nephew and heir in 1860. They are a reminder that the whole of this area, including Llyn Tegid, belonged to the Williams Wynn family of Wynnstay, Ruabon. They once owned so much land in North Wales that they were known as the 'Princes *in* Wales ', but on the death of the 7th baronet in 1944 the high death duties resulted in the great Glanllyn estate being transferred to the Treasury in lieu of death duties. The mansion of Glanllyn, which overlooks the lake, is now an Outward Bound School for the Urdd Gobaith Cymru (Welsh League of Youth) as their summer camp.

At Pennantlliw, north-west of Llanuwchllyn (also part of the Glanllyn estate), the Dolhendre Scheme to arrest rural depopulation was inaugurated as part of the Festival of Britain celebrations in 1951. An account of this imaginative scheme, planned by the Welsh Committee, is given in Welsh and English in a booklet *The Dolhendre Scheme: An Experiment in Rural Reconstruction* by Wyn Ll. Griffith. A group of old stone upland farms and cottages was modernized and others were built to blend with the traditional styles, for Forestry Commission workers.

Between Llanuwchllyn and Plas Glanllyn is Caer-gai, on a slope north of the A.494. The 17th century mansion is on the site of an earlier house, destroyed in the Civil War, which was the birthplace of Rowland Vaughan, poet, translator and royalist. The estate remained in the family until 1740 when it was bought by Sir Watkin Williams Wynn, the 3rd baronet. Incorporated in each wing of Caer-gai is a stone slab on which are carved Welsh verses by the Cavalier poet. Excavations have revealed part of the site of the Roman fort of Caer-gai, the main part of which lies beneath the foundations of the house. It has associations with Cei Hir, the Sir Kay of Arthurian legends, and his father Sir Ector, one of the most noble of the knights of the Round Table.

Some of the greatest Welsh patriots and advocates of

the Welsh language have been born in the near neighbourhood of Llanuwchllyn. The Rev. Robert Thomas (Ap Fychan), who was born at Tŷ Coch, Pennantlliw-bach in 1809, was an Independent minister and tutor, poet and man of letters whose bardic name was chosen because, although his family was pitifully poor, he was descended from the Vaughans of Caer-gai. He was a loyal friend of the Rev. Michael Daniel Jones, son of the first Principal of the Independent College founded at Llanuwchllyn in 1841. Michael Jones was born in the manse of the 17th century Yr Hen Gapel in 1822. After some years as a minister in the United States he succeeded his father as Principal of the Independent College, then at Bodiwan, Bala. He was an uncompromising patriot and a born fighter and his years at the College were marked by bitter controversy, which finally resulted in its removal to Bangor, but he is now probably better remembered as the leading spirit in the founding of the Welsh colony in Patagonia, which celebrated its centenary in 1965 when a plane-load of people flew from Wales to take part in the ceremonies.

The story of the hardships overcome by the colonists is little known outside Wales. The *Mimosa* sailed from Liverpool with 153 emigrants on board, including women and children, who left their Welsh homes as much from dire poverty as from their longing for freedom to speak their own language and live their own way of life, at a time when great landlords were exerting pressure to induce their Welsh tenants to become wholly English-speaking, then considered more progressive.

The colonists landed on the inhospitable coast of Patagonia and named the place Madryn, but they suffered so many vicissitudes in the first three years that their number was reduced to 90. In spite of this they held regular religious services, Sunday Schools, literary meetings and eisteddfodau, and even published a monthly hand-written newspaper - all in Welsh.

They managed to penetrate inland to the Chubut

Valley and to build a dam across the river, which enabled them to irrigate their crops. More emigrants arrived and their new capital, Rawson, was established on a firm basis. A Charter had been drawn up before leaving Wales under which, by agreement with the then Argentine Government, they had complete self-government, and women over the age of 18 were given the vote, although no women had a vote in the United Kingdom before 1918, and then only women over 30.

Welsh people are now in a minority in Patagonia and only partially self-governing. Spanish is now compulsory in the schools but there are still more than 5,000 who speak Welsh and maintain ties with Wales, although many of the younger generation now feel their first loyalty is to Argentina.

Coed-y- pry, a small stone house, now rebuilt, in Cwm Cynllwyd under Aran Benllyn, was the birthplace in 1858 of an equally patriotic Welshman and advocate of the Welsh language, Owen Morgan Edwards, one of the best-loved scholars of his age. In his early school-days Owen Edwards suffered from the 'Welsh Not', the iniquitous practice of giving any child speaking Welsh, either during lessons or in the school playground, some token which he had to hold until he could detect another child letting fall a Welsh word. It was largely due to these humiliations that he made it his life's work to improve the status of the Welsh language and to inspire his countrymen and women with a love of the Welsh tongue. He was appointed the first Chief Inspector of Schools in 1907, under the new Welsh Education Department, and made great reforms in the whole system of education, not least by encouraging the use of the Welsh language. He never spared himself in the pursuit of his official duties and was equally unflagging in writing books and articles on Welsh history and literature, and in translating Welsh classics into English for those who could not read the originals.

His work as author, editor and educationalist has been one of the chief factors in the renewed interest and pride in the Welsh language and literature.

It has been said that he viewed history with an artist's eye rather than through a researcher's microscope, and it is true that whilst the great Welsh scholars of the Bangor School founded by Sir John Morris-Jones were writing for other scholars, Owen Edwards was popularising history and literature in both English and Welsh in his own delightful prose. He founded magazines in both languages with a view to giving young writers an opening for contributions in poetry and prose.

He was knighted in 1916 and died in 1920, still in harness, at Llanuwchllyn, where he is buried.

Sir Owen's son, Sir Ifan ab Owen Edwards, was also a tireless worker on behalf of the Welsh language. He founded the first all-Welsh school in 1939 and the Urdd Gobaith Cymru (Welsh League of Youth) in 1922. In the words of its own declaration 'The Urdd believes that all Welshmen, whether Welsh-speaking or not, can grow to full stature and contribute to the welfare of the peoples of the world only by having their roots in their own historical tradition, and inheriting that wonderfully rich culture of the democracy that is Wales'. It is a national youth organization which receives support from all sections of the Welsh nation and the State, and recognition from other Youth movements all over the world. It is non-political and non-sectarian and exchanges visits with young people overseas. It holds an annual National Youth Eisteddfod, and an annual Mabolgampau (Youth Games) is organized.

MAENTWROG, in the Vale of Ffestiniog, at an important road junction, derives its name from the 'Stone of Twrog', a glacier-borne granitic boulder, unlike any in the locality, which is in the churchyard. No one really knows how it got there but one ancient tradition says that St. Twrog, son of a 6th century Prince in Armorica (present day Brittany), hurled it down from a mountain on to a heathen altar in the valley.

Although the church is of early foundation, it was rebuilt in 1896. It has an elaborate Oakley memorial and other monuments to the Oakley family of Tan-y-bwlch, whose name was changed by marriage more than once in the course of the centuries.

Maentwrog was built largely by William Oakley in the early Victorian era. The houses with their wooden galleries against their background of wooded cliffs, with mountains dominating the view on the north, are reminiscent of those in a Tyrolese village. There is a fine old bridge across the Afon Dwyryd to the picturesque, gabled Oakley Arms, also built by the Oakley family.

Plas Tan-y-bwlch, a large Victorian 'castle' with embattled walls, mullioned windows and an arched gatehouse, was the home of the Oakley family, of whom W.G. Oakley won awards from the Society of Arts for reclaiming good cornland from inundation in the years before the now better-known A.W. Madocks began building his embankment across the Glaslyn estuary.

The Oakley family ventured into the slate quarrying industry and did a considerable amount of building in the neighbourhood in addition to Maentwrog. In 1824 they were involved in a lawsuit with Lord Rothschild, who had been granted a monopoly of mineral rights in the Welsh hills and had trespassed on Oakley land, but eventually the High Court action went to the Oakleys by default.

Maentwrog's list of rectors goes back to the 14th century. The most distinguished was Archdeacon Edmund Prys, who was inducted in 1572. He was 'conspicuous for his manifold learning', and assisted Bishop Morgan in the translation of the Bible into Welsh. His *Salmau Cân*, a metrical version of the Psalms, was the first Welsh book in which music was printed, and is still used in Wales. He lived at Tyddyn Du, now a farmhouse, near Gellilydan, on the old road to Trawsfynydd.

The daughter of a later rector became the wife of

Thomas Love Peacock, the novelist and poet. Peacock first visited Maentrog in January 1810 and wrote enthusiastically to his friend, Edward Hooker, that he had taken up his residence 'in the land of all that is beautiful in nature, and all that is lovely in women'. He also described it as 'enchanting even in winter: in summer it must be a terrestrial paradise'. In another letter he promised that when Hooker visited him in August, he would show him 'scenes of such exquisite beauty and of such overpowering sublimity, as once beheld can never be forgotten'.

Although Peacock does not appear to have liked the Welsh men he met, he admired the women and fell in love with Jane Gruffydd, describing her as 'the most innocent, the most amiable, the most beautiful girl in existence', but it was not until eight years after he last saw her, upon securing employment in India House and a secure future, that he wrote to propose to her - and she accepted him. Peacock's novel, *The Misfortunes of Elphin*, is founded on Welsh traditions and some of his other novels have a Welsh setting.

MALLWYD, almost on the south-east border of the Snowdonia National Park, is a mile south of Dinas Mawddwy on the A.470 in the upper valley of the Dyfi, at its junction with the A.458 from Welshpool in Powys.

The ancient church, much restored in 1914, has a massive oak lintel over the south door, dated 1641, with a rib and skull above it (found in the neighbourhood) which are said to be those of a prehistoric animal. There is a memorial to Dr. John Davies, who was rector of Mallwyd for 40 years in the early 17th century. He was one of the greatest of Welsh scholars. He published a Welsh Grammar in 1621 and a Welsh-Latin Dictionary in 1632 which together laid a firm foundation for later studies in the Welsh language. He is also believed to have been largely responsible for the correctness of the language in Bishop Parry's translation of the Bible into

Welsh. Dr. Davies's wife was a grand-daughter, on her mother's side, of Baron Lewis Owen, who had been murdered by the Red Bandits of Mawddwy, traditions of whose ruthless exploits survive and whose memory is kept alive in the name of the 18th century Red Bandits Inn.

George Borrow thought Mallwyd a 'small but pretty village', and enjoyed his night's stay there, in contrast to his view of Dinas Mawddwy which he had disliked, although he had rapturously saluted 'Aber Cywarth' in the belief that it was there Ellis Wynne of Y Las Ynys, near Harlech, had written his immortal book *Gweledigaetheu y Bardd Cwsc* (The Visions of the Sleeping Bard). Although Ellis Wynne's son William was curate of Mallwyd between 1731 and 1733, the book had been published in London in 1703, and there is no evidence to support Borrow's claim that it was in Abercywarch he wrote his masterpiece.

West and north of Mallwyd is the beautiful Dyfi Forest which, with the Dyfi-Corris Forest, covers some 30 square miles in the valleys of the Dyffryn and Dysynni. The Forestry Commission began planting there in 1926 and the many trees now flourishing include plantations of Lawson's cypress, western red cedar, a fine plot of Chilian beech and a stand of western hemlock, believed to be the finest in Europe.

A Forestry Commission road from Aberangell, in Cwm Dyfi, south of Mallwyd, climbs Black Hendry, and forest paths follow the winding of the Afon Angell.

PENRHYNDEUDRAETH, as its name implies, is on a headland between two beaches at the meeting of the A.487 and the A.4085. It has a station on British Rail (W.R.) and another on the Ffestiniog Railway.

The nucleus of broad streets and large open squares was planned in the Victorian era by the local squire, David Williams, and Holy Trinity church was built in 1858, but there is modern ribbon development along the

Porthmadog road.

PORTMEIRION, on a thickly wooded rocky peninsula jutting out between the estuaries of the Dwyryd and Glaslyn, on the north coast of the Traeth Bach, is the realization of an architect's dream. Sir Clough Williams-Ellis, who has spent his long life fighting the desecration of Britain's landscape by unimaginative 'developments', said in a broadcast during his 91st year that he had cherished the idea of creating a village embodying his own ideas for many years. He had sought all over the world for a suitable site until, quite by chance, he found exactly what he needed within a few miles of his home, Plas Brondanw.

Although Sir Clough had Porto Fino in mind as a basis, Portmeirion developed on original lines. He adapted the beautiful site and collected gates, fireplaces, plaster-work, ceilings, wood and stone carvings, and other carefully chosen items from old houses far and near which were being demolished, and created a place of outstanding charm and individuality.

Among writers who found Portmeirion an ideal place in which to work were Noel Coward, who wrote *Blithe Spirit* in the Watch Tower, Bernard Shaw and Bertrand Russell. Portmeirion has also been a base for making several films, including the *Inn of the Seventh Happiness*, starring Ingrid Bergman, and for the popular T.V. series *The Prisoner.*

The Gwillt Garden at Portmeirion has been planted with knowledge and discrimination by Caton Haigh, an authority on Himalayan flowering trees and shrubs.

Portmeirion is on private land and a fee is charged to day visitors.

TAL-Y-LLYN. The enchanting little lake of Tal-y-llyn lies in a deep hollow below the precipitous heights of Cadair Idris and is skirted on the south-east by the B.4405. The tiny hamlet is on the south-west shore, where the Afon Dysynni flows out of the lake. The very early 17th century church has a 13th century timber roof to the nave and Tudor panels in the chancel roof, painted with red and white roses, with faces on the intersections. A cross in the churchyard marks the grave of a Scotswoman, Jennie Jones, who 'was with her husband of the 23rd Royal Welch Fusiliers at the Battle of Waterloo and was on the field three days'.

TRAWSFYNYDD.

The village of Trawsfynydd is 800ft. above sea level, on the A.470 which runs north from Dolgellau. It is on the south-east of Llyn Trawsfynydd, the reservoir of the Corporation of Liverpool, which is three miles long and a mile wide. It is a favourite haunt of anglers.

There is a striking statue in the main street of Ellis Humphrey Evans (Hedd Wyn) 'the Shepherd Poet', who was born in 1887 at the farmstead of Yr Ysgwin, just outside the village. He won many prizes for his poetry before joining the Royal Welch Fusiliers at the outbreak of the 1914-18 war. He entered the Chair competition at Birkenhead in 1917, which he won, but was killed in action just before the result was announced. The Chair was draped in black, and the occasion is remembered as Y Gadair Ddu (The Black Chair) eisteddfod.

The restored church of Trawsfynydd has a 16th century arcade of octagonal wooden pillars and has numerous brass and slate memorials.

The first inland nuclear power station in Britain, designed by Sir Basil Spence, was built on the north-east of the lake and blends reasonably well with the surrounding mountains, by which it is dwarfed.

Two miles away, on a hill 250ft. above the power station, is the Tomen-y-Mur, the site of a small Roman fort on the road north from Maridunum which was garrisoned from about A.D.78 to A.D.140. It had a brick or pottery kiln attached to it, which is one of only three yet found in Wales, and is neighboured by traces of a small Roman amphitheatre, showing as irregularities in a field. There are only seven other Roman amphitheatres in the whole of Britain, and the one at Tomen is said to be the only one attached to an auxiliary fort.

Tomen-y-Mur may have been a stronghold of the chieftains of Ardudwy after the departure of the Romans, and is associated with the Mur Castell of *The Mabinogion* story of *Math, son of Mathonwy*, in which Blodeuedd is created by the magician Gwydion from 'the flowers of the oak, the flowers of the broom, and the flowers of the meadowsweet'.

The Trawsfynydd Tankard found in the neighbourhood is an outstanding example of Celtic art. It is now in the Liverpool Museum.

The Normans built a small circular motte and bailey on the mound, which was the place of assembly of an English expedition led by William Rufus in November 1095. It was forced to retreat to Chester owing to atrocious weather. Twenty years later the site was a rendezvous for the expedition led by Henry I against Gruffydd ap Cynan.

TYWYN, three miles north-west of Aberdyfi on the A.493, is on level green fields beside a fine sandy bathing beach where there are several caravan parks. The older part of the town lies nearly a mile inland, backed by mountains.

The parish church, although rather over-restored, is still of exceptional interest. The greater part is of genuine Norman work, although some parts are reproductions, and it has a famous monument, St.Cadfan's Stone, 7ft. high, with an inscription which Sir John Morris-Jones believed dated from the 7th century, but Dr.Nash-Williams said more cautiously 'from the 7th to the 9th century'. It is the earliest monument inscribed in the Welsh language. In spite of its name, the stone has no association with St.Cadfan, who Christianized the district and founded a clas (a cloister or community) at

155

Tywyn in the 6th century.

Tywyn became the Mother church of all Meirionydd south of the Afon Dysynni, and had an abbot until 1171. It was still served by a group of clerics in 1291. Its wealth and privileges were celebrated in the mid-13th century by Llywelyn Fardd, in *Canu Gadfan,* in which he describes the 'lofty fane of Cadfan, by the margin of the blue sea', and praises the hospitality of the abbot.

Tywyn church also has a 14th century effigy of the Knight of Dolgoch and Ynysmaengwyn, Gruffydd Adda, and the effigy of a mass priest remarkable for the amice worn on the head as a hood instead of being folded around the neck.

Huw Ellis, who was born at Trawsfynydd in 1714, is buried in the churchyard. He was a skilled player of the 'telyn deir-res' (triple harp) and was considered the best Welsh folk-song player of his time. He was drowned accidentally in the Afon Dysynni in 1774.

Ynysmaengwyn estate, which was inherited by the Corbet family in the 17th century, is north of Tywyn, at the mouth of the Afon Dysynni. It was almost entirely reclaimed from wasteland by William Corbet who was also one of the first Welsh landowners to improve stock breeding. Ynysmaengwyn was sold in 1874 to John Corbett, M.P., of Impney, near Droitwich, a wealthy self-made salt manufacturer and philanthropist. In spite of the similarity in the name, he was not connected by blood with the original Corbets.

The Corbett Arms Hotel, in Corbett Square, formerly the Corbet Arms, a plain but handsome building, was already in existence for many years before the Ynysmaengwyn estate was sold; but the Market Hall, with its clock tower, cupola and Dutch gables, was given to the town by John Corbett, who also built the sea wall and esplanade.

Tradition says that an earlier house on the site of Plas Ynysmaengwyn was burnt down during the Civil War after Cromwell had been refused accommodation for himself and his soldiers and their horses, but whether by the Parliamentarians or by the occupants is not clear.

The mid-18th century house on the same site was built by Anne Corbet, the heiress of Ynysmaengwyn, who married Athelstane Owen of Rhiwsaeson, Montgomeryshire. The latter took the name of Corbet. During the 1939-45 war the whole estate was taken over by the military authorities and used as a training centre for troops, and in 1948 the estate was presented to the County of Meirionydd by Miss Mary Corbett.

Plas Dolaugwyn, just off the road between Tywyn and Abergwynolwyn, was referred to in a document of 1620 as 'the new house of the said Lewys Gwyn in the parish of Towyn called "Y Dole Gwyn".' Lewis Gwyn figures in a number of cywyddau by 17th century bards. The Gwyns had family connections with the Corbets but, if tradition is correct, this did not prevent them from giving hospitality to Cromwell and his men after they had been turned away from Ynysmaengwyn - or possibly they feared that their house would also be burnt down.

Tywyn has three railway stations - one British Rail (W.R.), and the other two on the Tal-y-llyn Railway, which has its south-western terminus and headquarters at Tywyn. The Tal-y-llyn Railway Museum at Wharf Station has a fine display of steam locomotives, rolling stock, equipment and mementoes of the narrow-gauge railways of Great Britain and Ireland, including a horse-hauled slate wagon from Nantlle tramway and a peculiar 'host wagon' from the Padarn Railway which was a precursor of the containerized transport of to-day.

The Tal-y-llyn railway was opened in 1865 for the transport of slate by steam-hauled locomotives. It has a gauge of 2ft. 3ins. and a maximum gradient of 1 in 60. Passengers were first carried in 1867 and it has operated continuously since then. It is the first narrow gauge railway in the world able to celebrate a hundred years of steam operation without a break.

When the quarries closed, the railway only survived

through the efforts of Sir Henry Haydn Jones, its owner and general manager. It escaped nationalization in 1947 and when Sir Henry died in 1950, at the age of 87, it was taken over immediately by a band of railway enthusiasts. They were the pioneers of railway preservation and, incidentally, the inspiration for the comedy film, *The Titfield Thunderbolt,* made by Ealing Studios with a certain amount of artistic and comic licence. L.T.C. Rolt, who acted as General Manager for the first two years, gives a fascinating account of the many difficulties overcome by the Tal-y-llyn Railway Preservation Society in its early days in his book *Railway Adventure.*

Between 1900 and 1905 the Tal-y-llyn Railway had a contract with the Postmaster General for the conveyance of a sealed mailbag between Tywyn and Abergwynolwyn, and a private posting bag for the quarries. In 1957, the Preservation Society issued miniature sheets of railway letter stamps, and other issues followed, all depicting the little trains and their engines. A special First Day Cover was issued for the centenary, postmarked with a facsimile of the cancellation of 5th July, 1865, the day on which the Act of Parliament by which it was incorporated received the Royal Assent.

The Society's workshops are at Pentre station, near Corbett Square, Tywyn, from which the line runs up Cwm Fathew to Rhydyronen, where there is one of the best chalybeate springs in Britain, to Brynglas for the pretty walk beside the stream to the Dolgoch waterfalls and the mansion of Dolaugwyn. The line continues on to Abergwynolwyn, the mountain ringed village on the B.4405, three miles south of Tal-y-llyn lake. Abergwynolwyn was the upper terminus of the Tal-y-llyn railway until the recent three-quarters of a mile extension to Nant Gwernol.

North of Tywyn is Morfa Camp, an Army Outward Bound school, and Tonfanau British Rail station, on the other side of the Dysynni estuary, but the A.493 turns inland, bridging the Afon Fathew at Bryn-crug and the

Afon Dysynni near the farmhouse of Tal-y-bont, which marks the site of a mansion belonging to Llywelyn the Great. It was from here that he wrote letters to the Archbishop of Canterbury and other notable people. Twenty years later Edward I dated a charter from here.

Just beyond the farmhouse the road again turns back to the coast and runs parallel with the British Rail track to Llangelynin. The small, barnlike 12th century church of St.Celynin is on a natural cliff terrace below the road. It has a 15th century tie-beam roof, with two mid-19th century chandeliers, faint remains of frescoes and an elor-feirch (double horse bier) with shafts at either end, enabling horses to convey coffins over the steep hillsides. There is a similar bier at Llangower.

The names, titles and addresses of the holders can be seen on the plain 19th century benches which form the only seating. Services are still held there occasionally.

A slate in the churchyard, near the porch, marks the grave of Abram Wood, the 18th century 'King of the Gypsies', who is said to have been a 'splendid fiddler'. He was the patriarch of the largest tribe of gipsies in Wales, which for many generations provided the Principality with a remarkable line of brilliant harpists. John Sampson, Librarian of Liverpool University, compiled a detailed history and genealogy of the Wood family. He believed Abram Wood was 100 years old at the time of his death in 1799.

Road and rail continue north along the coast to Llwyngwril, a pretty village on one of the foothills of the Cadair Idris range. On the south are the remains of a prehistoric hill-fort, Castell-y-Gaer, and beside a path leading down to the sea is a small, dry-walled Quaker burial ground, with the date 1646 over the entrance. There were numerous Quaker families in the neighbourhood in the 17th century, among whom were the Humphreys of Llwyn-du, one of whom married Ellis ap Rees of Brynmawr, Dolgellau, and became the mother of Rowland Ellis. The Llwyngwril Quakers suffered considerable persecution, and a number of them emigrated to Pennsylvania. Part of their burial ground is now used by the Methodists.

North of Llwyngwril the foot hills of Cadair Idris rise sheer from the sea, and the road to Fairbourne, like the railway, is modern and much exposed to the Atlantic gales. The old road north went over the mountains by the Ffordd Ddu to Dolgellau.

INDEX

163

164

166

167